INSIDE THIS

HERE TODAY!
AND
GONE TOMORROW!

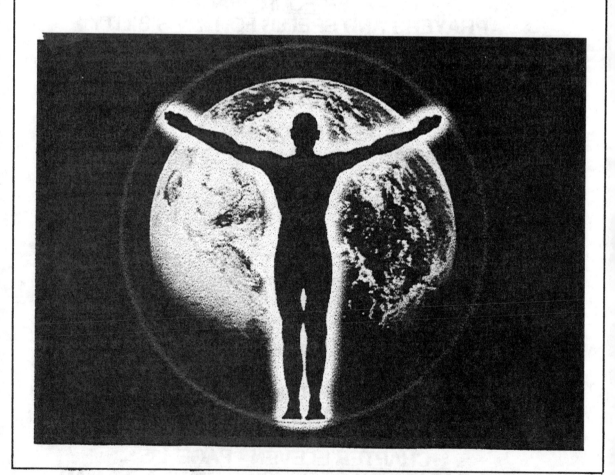

Commander X

INVISIBILITY AND LEVITATION:
How-To Keys To
Personal Performance

ABELARD PRODUCTIONS PUBLISHING

ISBN: 0-938294-36-9

Front Cover Design by Chris Fleming
Back Cover Art by Carol Ann Rodriguez
Editorial Direction by Tim Beckley
and Tim Swartz

For foreign or other rights contact:
GLOBAL COMMUNICATIONS
Box 753, New Brunswick, NJ 08903

INVISIBILITY AND LEVITATION

Introduction by Timothy Green Beckley

Since time is so precious to me, I have to work ten to twelve hours a day, sometimes under very trying conditions. The phone rings, someone is at the door, there is a business meeting or lunch that I have to go to. The outcome is that often nothing seems to get accomplished, or done on time.

If I didn't "steal" a moment here or there, deadlines would fly right out the window, and our little publishing empire would go bust. Traveling on the bus or train between New Jersey and New York offers me a possibility to "catch up," but in order to do any serious editing or writing while on the move, its necessary to "stretch out" and utilize as much space as possible.

As cramped as a bus or train is, it's hard to concentrate or get anything done if you have a fellow commuter taking up the seat next to you. Chances are you're going to get elbowed every few minutes, or worse yet, someone is trying to get your opinion on the Dow Jones or current mortgage rates.

How can you be expected to get anything done under such trying circumstances? Obviously, you can't post a big sign next to you that says "OFF LIMITS, DO NOT DISTURB." Other commuters have the same rights as you do to find a seat.

The trick, as I've discovered, is to make yourself invisible so that those walking up and down the isle completely bypass the section of seats where you have made yourself comfortable. Simply "erase yourself" from existence and have them "move on," and you'll have plenty of opportunity to get some much needed work done.

This seems to work pretty good for me, and I think anyone can learn the process.

INVISIBILITY AND LEVITATION

The fact is, that over the years I've developed my powers so that when I don't want to be disturbed, I can make the seat next to me and even those across from where I am, completely "out of bounds."

I create a particular situation so that it's as if I don't even exist nor does anything around me. My mind sets the limitations and if I decided to "open up," I can literally "clear the air" at some point and make myself visible to others. Sometimes, if I'm in the right mood, I can even attract a pretty traveler to take the seat next to me and start a conversation.

The bottom line is that I'm not at the mercy of others. I've learned (at least to some degree) to set the ground rules. I would have to say that a lot has to do with my ability to make myself felt or unfelt, whatever the case may be depending upon the degree of pressure I'm under.

This is not to say that I can snap my fingers and turn into a cloud of smoke, but for what I've come to learn, apparently other people with a bit more training can take this process further and literally vanish in front of the eyes of others.

There are those, I'm convinced, who are not bound by earthly laws that most mortals have make for themselves. These adepts and avatars, if you want to call them that, have learned to do things which most of us can only dream of.

■ They can make themselves invisible.

■ They can leave the ground and travel in the air by levitating their physical form.

INVISIBILITY AND LEVITATION

In this book we will talk not only about those who have performed what seem to be miracles (after all Jesus did walk on water, and he did vanish into the clouds). We will also concentrate on how such miracles can work for all of us to better our lives and to raise our consciousness. That, after all, is the purpose of our understanding and applying the formulas known in previous ages only to the masters. For now we are entering the New Age of Enlightenment, and our "talents" and abilities will soon blossom forth according to our own individual spiritual development.

Interestingly enough, much of what we still consider to be "supernatural" was common place in the past such as on the sunken continents of Atlantic and Mu, and from what we know about our extraterrestrial "Space Brother" friends, levitation and invisibility are performed with the greatest of ease as a matter of course throughout the universe.

Timothy Green Beckley
Global Communications

THE QUEST FOR INSTANT INVISIBILITY

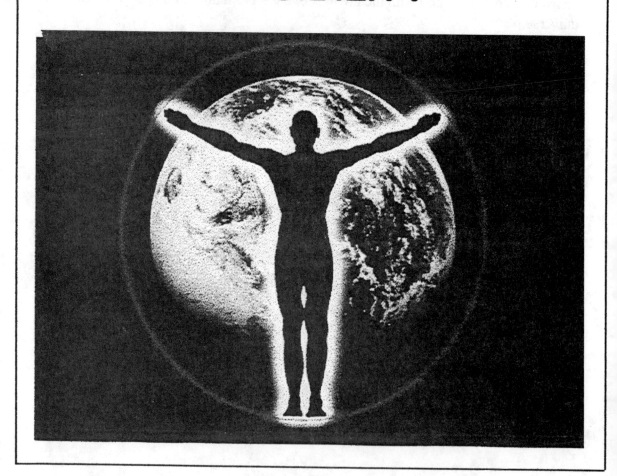

INVISIBILITY AND LEVITATION

Out of all the magical secrets that mankind has sought over the ages, probably the two most universal desires would be the ability to become invisible, and to levitate at will. Countless spells, incantations, potions, and talismans have been created, all with the purpose to achieve the goals of invisibility and unaided flight.

Many people today would scoff at the notion that one can become invisible, or fly with the help of magical or occult powers. However, ancient wisdom passed down from antiquity indicates that such "powers" are available if one only knows the true secrets of the lost wisdom of the ages.

These secrets, some which have been lost for centuries, have now been gathered together from the four corners of the Earth. With the new millennium, the time is now right for these lost teachings to be revealed to those willing to take on the great responsibility that such incredible powers can endow on an individual.

But be warned. Such powers can command a high price to those who would use them for evil purposes or for selfish gains. Powers such as these are not to be trifled with. The universe has its own built in safety mechanisms, ready to take down those who would trifle with the laws of the cosmos.

For those who would use these abilities on a quest for knowledge, or to help their fellow man, then they will find their path is readily before them, with guides and assistance to help them along their spiritual journey.

THE DREAM OF INVISIBILITY

Wouldn't it be nice to be able to disappear upon command? Think of all the

INVISIBILITY AND LEVITATION

absolutely incredible things that you could do if you weren't visible to the human eye. You could walk into a room undetected. You could listen to others as they converse in private. You'd be able to visit friends and foe alike without having them know that they were being "spied" upon. You could visit the theater, the movies, a ball game and stand or sit anywhere you wanted, even back stage.

If you were dishonest, you could even walk into a bank and walk out with a sack full of money and the cash wouldn't be missed until you were safely home. How many of us, if able to become invisible, could resist the temptation of abusing the power. Who among us can say they wouldn't succumb to voyeuristic fantasies, or theft if we knew we could get away with it. Even murder could become so much more easy if the power of invisibility became readily available.

For these reasons and others, the ancient knowledge of invisibility have been a closely guarded secret. Known only by those with the most pure of heart and soul. Masters of universal truths and the mysteries of the human mind.

Throughout history there have been those individuals who claim that they can make their flesh and bones "fade" from view. These master adepts use mystical, metaphysical or occult powers. They are advanced humans who have discovered various techniques that give them supernatural powers. Some of them have used magick, others have superior mental abilities. It seems hard to believe, but apparently it is possible to learn such techniques yourself. Some say the secret of invisibility can be learned relatively quickly. Others maintain that it takes years of study and purification of the mind. Some say it happens by accident. Others claim that they can make themselves vanish upon command.

Human invisibility has been written about for centuries. Indo-European and pre-Aryan shamanistic beliefs accompanied the peoples who eventually migrated into the Indus Valley in approx. 2,500-1,500 BCE. Here, men and women of great spiritual attainment, and extraordinary powers came to be called Rishis. The Vedas, which form the basis of Hinduism, came from the teachings of the Rishis. These teachings offer descriptions of the rituals and techniques of the Hindu priests.

Later in Hinduism, we find the secret doctrines called the Upanishads. Within the writings there is a section called the "Yogatattva," which gives the rich mystical philosophy of the discipline and theory of practice for attaining knowledge of the essence of God. A serious student of raja yoga was taught that certain supernormal powers, called Siddhas, were a natural outcome of gaining mastery over one's mind and environment, and were used as valuable indications of the student's spiritual progress. One of these yogic Siddhas was human invisibility.

Patanjali, author of the Yoga-sutra, one of the earliest documents among the early Indian writings, described the process to produce human invisibility. He said that concentration and meditation can make the body imperceptible to other men, and "a direct contact with the light of the eyes no longer existing, the body disappears." The light engendered in the eye of the observer no longer comes into contact with the body that has become invisible, and the observer sees nothing at all. The mystery is how this could possibly occur, the explanation of the process of invisibility was most likely left up to the teacher to impart to the student directly.

MOSES - THE GREAT MAGICIAN

Most of us think of Moses as the man who led the Hebrews out of Egypt. The man who parted the waters of the Red Sea in order to drown the pursuing Pharaohs soldiers. However, according to Biblical references, Moses was also a great magician and seer. He was a mystic who understood and acted upon cosmic or universal laws. He was able to turn his staff into a snake, and he performed other amazing feats because he knew certain cosmic laws that were handed down to him by the Supreme Being.

INVISIBILITY AND LEVITATION

Jewish historians say that Moses was murdered by ambitious politicians, but it may be that Moses simply faded away when the time came for him to vanish. In the book, *Antiquities of the Jews*, the author Josephus writes, "As he went to the place where he was to vanish from their sight, they all followed after him weeping, but Moses beckoned with his hand to all who were remote from him, and then to stay behind in quiet. All those who accompanied him were the senate, and Eleazar, the High Priest, and Joshua, their commander. As soon as they were come to the mountain called Abarim, Moses dismissed the senate, and a cloud stood over him on the sudden, and he disappeared."

There are those that assume that Moses ascended into Heaven, just as Christ did. However, there is some debate regarding this issue. H. Spencer Lewis, founder and first Imperator of the Rosicrucian Order, believed that the cloud referred to was a mystical cloud and that Moses and Jesus actually disappeared, possibly into another dimension.

Oliver Leroy, a noted authority on religion says that in his study of Catholic Saints, "It is possible to account for the vanishing of a levitated person...not by the incredible heights reached...in his ascent...but by a phenomenon of invisibility, some instances of which are to be found in the lives of several Saints."

SURROUNDED IN A CLOUD

There is something about a dark cloud that invokes thoughts of mystery. Entire army regiments have been known to disappear inside clouds. In 1915, during World War I the Allies were attempting to capture Constantinople (now known as Istanbul). The Allies had landed at different points on the Gallipoli peninsula, meeting strong Turkish resistance. Some months later Gen. Sir Ian Hamilton moved new troops secretly to Suvia Bay on the Aegean coast.

INVISIBILITY AND LEVITATION

During the afternoon of August 28 the weather over Suvia Bay was clear except for a group of dark clouds that hovered over Hill 60 about three-fourths of a mile from the front. Despite a breeze of four or five miles an hour from the south, the clouds maintained their position. At ground level below them was another light gray cloud about 800 feet long, 200 feet high and 200 feet wide. It seemed almost solid and hung over a sunken road in a dry creek.

On Rhododendron Spur, about a mile and a half southwest of Hill 60 and some 300 feet higher, were stationed 22 New Zealand soldiers of Number Three Section of Number One Field Company. They noted the strange ground-level cloud as a British regiment began marching up the sunken road toward Hill 60.

The regiment was the British First Fourth Norfolk, several hundred men. The observers watched as the troops marched right into the cloud. However, no one was seen to come out. About an hour later the cloud gently rose from the ground and joined the clouds above it. Thereupon, all the clouds moved northward towards Bulgaria and disappeared from view.

When Turkey surrendered in 1918, the British immediately demanded return of the regiment. But the Turks maintained that they had never heard of the regiment nor had they captured any of its members. Apparently the British soldiers had disappeared forever within the mysterious cloud. Cases such as this have been well documented and can be found in many books and journals.

Recently, a Canadian mystic, Richard Maurice Bucke, had a similar experience. He stated that without warning he found himself wrapped in a flame-colored cloud. For a moment he thought there was a fire nearby, but then he realized that the light was from within himself. He felt a sense of exultation, of joyousness, accompanied by an intellectual illumination quite impossible to describe. He realized that at that moment he could disappear entirely from this level of reality, but instead was able to maintain

INVISIBILITY AND LEVITATION

the mental discipline to keep himself from vanishing.

Bucke was so moved by this experience that he spent the rest of his life studying it. His special name for it was Cosmic Consciousness. Such self illumination is part of the practice of invisibility. According to many who have accomplished this seemingly remarkable feat, when the principles for how it can be applied are understood, the task is relatively easy.

CAN WE ACHIEVE INVISIBILITY?

Basically, there is no mystery about the subject. If we stand in a room that is completely dark, everything in it, including ourselves, is invisible. Shine a flashlight on the furniture and the parts that are lighted suddenly become visible. Because our eyes are light-sensitive organs, they pick up the reflected light from the object and we therefore see the object.

Not all objects reflect light. Some refract it and some absorb it. Some objects reflect light and also absorb it. White snow in sunlight absorbs very little light, which is why the sight of it may hurt your eyes. We don't have any trouble at all looking through glass because it is transparent, so much so that people who installed sliding glass doors in their homes were crashing into them until they decorated the glass with decals. The glass in the doors was actually invisible because it reflected little to no light at all.

Science fiction writers say that we could all become invisible if we could bend light waves around ourselves. If no light struck our bodies, no light would be reflected, and therefore we would not be seen. That's easier said than done. Light travels in a straight line. Until we can change that natural phenomenon we are not likely to achieve

14

INVISIBILITY AND LEVITATION

invisibility. However, maybe we can do it in another way.

HOW TO SEE YOUR AURA

Before we can hope to achieve invisibility we should be familiar with the aura that surrounds us, as it does all living things. The fact that an aura, a subtle and colorful emanation of energy that surrounds the body, truly exists was proved by Kirlian photography. These photographs clearly show the emanations, and it is alleged that one can tell if a part of the body is not working properly by the change in the aura's color and shape.

However, we don't need Kirlian photography to see our aura. We all have the natural ability to see the aura, all we need is a little patience. In his book *Invisibility*, (Aquarian Press), Steve Richards outlines the procedure by which aura visibility is possible.

You need a closet large enough for a chair. Use bath towels to seal the crack under the door to insure that no light enters. What you want is total darkness. Your left and right hands have different polarities. When you bring them together there is a flow of energy from one to the other. When the fingertips touch the aura is intensified. At that moment you should see your aura.

We don't want to mislead you into thinking this is a simple exercise. It is not. You won't see your aura the first time, you may not see it the fiftieth time. If you stay with it, you will eventually see it. Richards recommends that you put your hands together in the darkened closet just as you would if you were praying, palms touching. Then separate your palms, so that any energy that passes over from one hand to the other must center on your fingers.

INVISIBILITY AND LEVITATION

When the fingers are separated there will be a light produced by the magnetic energy passing from the fingers of one hand to the fingers of the other. An important point to remember here is that when you begin the exercise, **will** that you will see the light.

Discontinue the experiment after about ten minutes and try again the next day. Some experimenters have tried it for three or four months before succeeding. Don't become discouraged. Even if you don't succeed, the exercise will help to prepare you for the bigger achievement you desire - - - that of becoming invisible.

WHAT IS IN THE MYSTERIOUS MIST?

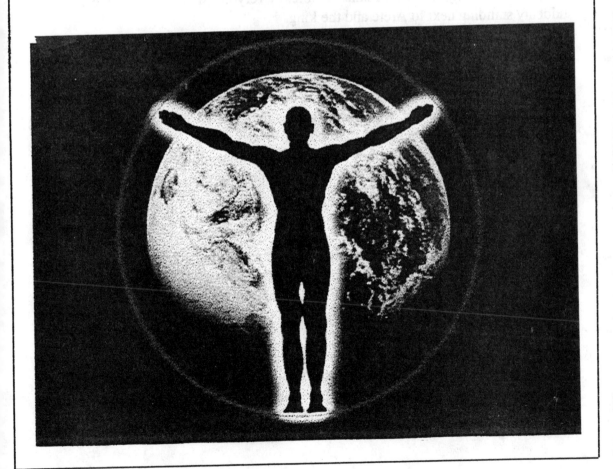

INVISIBILITY AND LEVITATION

Research of ancient texts and manuscripts indicates that whenever invisibility occurs in antiquity it is always accompanied by a cloud or mist. The ancient Greeks were well aware of it, and Homer and Hesiod mention the magical mists in their writings. In the *Odyssey*, when Odysseus washed ashore near the city of the Phaeacians, he wanted to get to the palace without being seen. Homer said that the problem was solved by the Goddess Athene, who "shed a deep mist about Odysseus" so that he would not be seen on his way into the palace. As Odysseus passed through the city he was hidden in a thick cloud of darkness.

Enveloped in his cloud of darkness, Odysseus went to the court and reached Arete and King Alcinous. He placed his hands on the knees of the queen, and at that instant the cloud fell away and he became visible. Everyone was stunned to see a man suddenly standing next to Arete and the king.

Homer also tells us that even as heroes were battling over Troy, Hera approached Zeus on Mount Ida to ask a favor. Zeus had his own favor to ask, a sexual one. Embarrassed, Hera said it was not possible, that there were too many gods and goddesses about. She suggested that they go to her room. Zeus had a better idea. They could have all the privacy they needed, through invisibility. Zeus then surrounded Hera and himself with a dense golden cloud, so thick that even the sun's rays could not penetrate it.

Hesiod, the ancient Greek poet wrote about the cloud in connection with the men of the Golden Age: "Now that the earth has gathered over this generation, these are called pure and blessed spirits. . . They mantle themselves in dark mist and wander all over the country."

Oddly, the English word *haze* comes from the Hebrew word *hazaz*, which referred to the "shining cloud that causes man to have visions." Cagliostro had in his possession a letter written to him by the Master of one of the Egyptian lodges. A passage read:

INVISIBILITY AND LEVITATION

"The first philosopher of the New Testament appeared without being called and gave the entire assemble, prostrate before the blue cloud in which he appeared, his blessing." Blue is one of the colors seen in the cloud, although it has also been described as being blue-gray.

The Romans have also been aware of the strange mist which signals the arrival or departure of one of authority. Dionysius told the story of Ilia, mother of Romulus and Remus. She was a Vestal Virgin and was ravished in a grove consecrated to the God Mars. Dionysius wrote:

"It is said by some that the act was committed by one of her loves to gratify his passion. Others make Amulius the author of it. But the greatest number give this fabulous account: that it was a specter, representing the god to whom the place was consecrated. They add that this adventure was attended, among other heavenly signs, with the eclipse of the sun, and a darkness spread over the heavens; that the specter far excelled the appearance of a man, both in beauty and in stature; and that the ravisher, to comfort the maiden, commanded her to be not at all concerned at what happened, since she had been united in marriage to the genius of the place. Having said this, he was wrapped in a cloud, and, being lifted from the earth, was borne upwards through the air."

Here we have a case of levitation and invisibility, just as it allegedly happened with Moses, Christ, some saints, and with holy men in nearly every religion.

Certain Spiritualists are capable of producing this cloud. It has been called *teleplasm* or *ideaplasm*, but the name invented by Charles Richet is *ectoplasm*. That's the name that stuck. It is now called ectoplasm by all students of the occult.

Richet made an in-depth study of the phenomenon. The substance ectoplasm is

19

reportedly produced by the body of a spirit medium. The ectoplasm flows from the mouths or other orifices of mediums while they are in a trance. The mediums can use this substance to make tables levitate, and sometimes this cotton candy like material can even form itself into a human-shaped apparition.

Richet was able to divide the formation of ectoplasm into three or four stages. At a seance the first stage included nothing visible, but there were rapping's heard. Objects moved about on their own, and sitters felt that they were being touched by an invisible hand. The second stage revealed the formation of a cloud. This is just barely visible. When the cloud becomes more luminous, Richet called it the third stage. At this point, a human nude shape started to form. The fourth state is one in which the complete human body is formed, or materialized.

The shape that emerges from the ectoplasm does not have to be human. It can be non-human, such as animals or flowers, or even an inanimate object such as jewelry or clothing.

Before you can hope to become invisible at will, you will have to master the art of producing ectoplasm. Don't be frightened off; it is not as hard as you might think.

The simplest way to produce ectoplasm is to imagine it forming into a common, everyday object. Try something simple at first, say a coin or a pencil. Find a quiet dimly lit room, sit and close your eyes. In your mind imagine that a cloud is forming into your object. Visualize the object becoming real. Try to mentally "feel" the object, its shape, its texture. Now imagine it on something in your house, a desk or table top. See it in your mind sitting on that desk or table. Visualize yourself going to that table and finding the coin there.

This experiment can take quite sometime before anything will happen. Total control

INVISIBILITY AND LEVITATION

Mediums have been producing what
is known as ectoplasm at seances for hundreds
of years in which "spirits" have been observed
to materialize into physical form.

of your mind is essential. If you find your mind is beginning to wander, stop for awhile and give yourself a break. You cannot force this kind of mental development. It takes time and practice.

Eventually you will be rewarded by actually finding the object you imagined. Probably it won't be in the exact same place you imagined it to be found. Instead, it will most likely turn up in a place you wouldn't expect to find something like it. Inside an old box, or an old coat pocket. Some practiced mediums and adepts have actually produced living beings with their mind powers. This is something that should not be attempted by a beginner, there are all sorts of pitfalls awaiting those who dabble recklessly with such powers.

THE INCREDIBLE PHENOMENON CALLED PALINGENESIS

Palingenesis is the materialization of a flower that has been cremated. A Polish doctor who lived in Cracovia delighted visitors by performing the feat. He had a set of small glasses, in each of which there were the ashes of a certain type of flower. His first step was to hold a glass over the flame of a candle. Soon the ashes would move, then rise up and disperse themselves inside the glass. Then a little dark cloud would appear and divide itself into many parts, all of which would finally represent the flower that had been cremated.

Madame Blavatsky, the famed mystic, wrote about the subject: "At a meeting of naturalists in 1834 in Stuttgart, a recipe for producing such experiments was found in a work of Oettinger. Ashes of burned plants contained in vials, when heated, exhibited again their various forms. A small, obscure cloud gradually rose in the vial, took a definite form, and presented to the eye the flower or plant the ashes consisted of. Oettinger wrote, 'The earthly husk remains in the retort, while the volatile essence ascends, like a spirit, perfect in form, but void in substance.'"

INVISIBILITY AND LEVITATION

The alchemists compared the phenomenon with the Phoenix, a mythical bird that rises from its ashes every 500 years and flies to the sun-temple at Heliopolus, where the Egyptians felt that its appearance was a favorable omen.

A man named Kircher resurrected a flower from its own ashes for Queen Christina of Sweden in 1687. He called himself an alchemist and noted that a person who wants to become an alchemist must have magnetic power to attract and coagulate invisible astral elements. We all have the magnetic power to some degree. This power can be enhanced with the right kinds of physical and mental exercises.

THE ROLE OF ALCHEMY IN INVISIBILITY

We desire to prolong and enjoy our lives, and we look to science for the answers. To prolong life in earlier eras the quest was for the Fountain of Youth. You can still see the so-called answers to long life in some advertising which promises you a ripe old age if you drink a certain sour milk, or eat bran cereal.

Today we equate the enjoyment of life with great wealth and material possessions, and there is no shortage of gimmicks to help you achieve riches. In the past, the love of easy living led to a search for the "Philosopher's Stone," which supposedly created wealth by the transmutation of base metals into gold.

Alchemy is often lumped in with Astrology and Sorcery, but as a science, it was developed at a much earlier date. Alchemists also enjoyed a superior knowledge. The beginning of alchemy is lost in antiquity. Some enthusiasts believe it began with the creation of man. Vincent de Beauvais felt that it at least went back to the days of Noah, who had to have been acquainted with alchemy in order to live to such a great age and to sire some 500 children.

INVISIBILITY AND LEVITATION

Researchers have traced alchemy to the Egyptians, from whom Moses was believed to have learned it. One study shows that the Chinese practiced it 2,500 years before Christ. The idea that metal can be changed to gold was toyed with in the Roman Empire, although the science did not really establish a foothold until the Eighth Century.

The Church banned it, and all classes of society dabbled in it. Unfortunately, there were some charlatans who gave alchemy a bad name. However, alchemy did play an important role in the history of humanity. It must not be judged by the charlatans who exploited it, but by the men who may now be deemed pioneers of civilization. These hard-working alchemists of long ago were the parents of modern science and physics. They also helped to adorn our literature and art. They have given to our language such words as crucible, amalgam, alcohol, potash, laudanum, precipitate, saturate, distillation, quintessence, affinity and many more.

Alchemists often stumbled upon discoveries they weren't searching for. The red oxide of mercury was such a discovery, as was nitric acid, nitrate of silver, the telescope, the magic lantern, gunpowder, the properties of gas, and laudanum. Believe it or not, it was the alchemists who first created the first medical clinic.

It is a misconception to think that the alchemists' only concern was to change metal into gold and to attain eternal youth. Those were only two phases of alchemy. Alchemy is actually the most occult of all occult sciences. The occult phenomena that we find so absorbing today was performed by them centuries ago. Alchemists dealt with autosuggestion, animal magnetism, hypnotism, telepathy, and ventriloquism long before these wonders were named.

Alchemist Abertus Magnus, for example, had the ability to mesmerize entire crowds just as Indian necromancers do at present. Cornelius Agrippa, another alchemist, at the request of Erasmus and other learned men called up from the grave many of the great

24

philosophers of antiquity, among them Cicero who, upon Agrippa's urging's, re-delivered his celebrated speech on Roscius. Agrippa also showed Lord Surrey in a reflection on a glass, the image of his mistress Geraldine. She was seen on a couch weeping for her lover. Lord Surry made a note of the exact time of the vision, and when he returned home, he learned that truly Geraldine was crying for him at the time he observed her in the magic glass.

When learning became popular again after the Renaissance, a mysterious sect rose up in Germany. Its members called themselves disciples of the Rosey Cross, or Rosicrucians. They claimed that they got their name from one Christian Rosencreutz. This man was supposedly initiated into the mysteries of the East during a pilgrimage to the Holy Land. The Rosicrucians' tenets were first made known to the world in the seventeenth century in an anonymous German work allegedly found in the tomb of Rosencreutz, who had died 120 years previously.

The legends that sprung up about him bordered on the astonishing. Researchers felt that the society began when it embraced the theories of Paracelsus and Dr. John Dee, who were the unrecognized founders of the Rosicrucians. In any event, the alchemists quickly accepted them.

The most important rule in the philosophy of the Rosicrucians was chastity. They could ignore hunger and thirst. They enjoyed perfect health and were able to prolong their lives indefinitely.

The earliest document that clearly mentions the Rosicrucians by name and purports to tell the story of its foundation, was called the *Fama Fraternitatis*. Written anonymously in German, the pamphlet was part of a larger Protestant treatise entitled in its first English translation: *The Universal and General Reformation of the Whole Wide World; Together with the Fama Fraternitatis of the Laudable Fraternity of the Rosy Cross, Written to all the Learned and the Rulers of Europe.*

INVISIBILITY AND LEVITATION

The manuscript probably began circulating around 1610, and the work was subsequently published in several languages. The first printed edition appeared in 1614 in the town of Kassel in western Germany.

Readers who desired to join in reforming the world were invited to "leave the old course, esteeming Popery, Aristotle, and Galen, yea and that which hath but a mere show of learning." The author asserted that no one could apply for membership directly, but would-be applicants might "speak either by word of mouth, or else. . .in writing. And this we say for a truth, that whosoever shall earnestly, and from his heart, bear affection unto us, will come to the fraternity's notice. And it shall be beneficial to him in goods, body, and soul."

In case anyone thought that the benefits might include lessons in practical alchemy, the author declared that "concerning the ungodly and accursed gold-making we do therefore by these presents publicly testify, that the true philosophers are far of another mind, esteeming little of the making of gold, which is but a subsidiary activity; for besides that, they have a thousand better things." Simply put, the Rosicrucians knew how to transform base metal into gold and how to make medicinal elixirs, and they could do either when it suited them, but their strongest alchemy was reserved for another, more laudable purpose: the transmutation of ordinary mortal intellect into spiritual and philosophical wisdom.

One of the hidden secrets of the alchemists and the Rosicrucians was the ability to make a living being invisible to "all around him." The knowledge to render a man invisible was revealed to a seventeenth-century French traveler named Paul Lucas. Lucas was traveling in what is now Turkey when he was introduced to a dervish, a monk in a mystic Muslim sect. "He was a man in every way extraordinary in learning," Lucas wrote after a long conversation with the dervish.

The dervish told Lucas about the "sublime science" and the quest for the philosophers' stone. The philosophers' stone could convey immortality upon its holder, as well as knowledge to "hide oneself away from all who would seek him." As proof, the dervish mentioned the name of Nicholas Flamel, one of France's most renowned alchemists and one who reportedly had possessed the stone. Flamel had lived in Paris during the latter half of the fourteenth century. He had amassed great wealth and had earned a saintly and enduring reputation by spending most of his fortune on charitable works. The dervish claimed that Flamel could "cover himself with a mist of darkness and that no locked door could keep him out."

Paul Lucas pointed out to the dervish that Flamel had died in 1417 at the age of eighty-seven. The dervish "smiled at my simplicity," Lucas wrote, "and asked, do you really believe this? No, no, my friend, Flamel is still living. It is not above three years since I left him in the Indies," he said. "He is one of my best friends." With that the dervish vanished completely before the astonished eyes of Lucas.

Alchemists believed that the philosophers' stone was a "stone which is not a stone." This substance, which carried literally hundreds of other names, such as the "powder of projection," the "virgins milk," and the "shade of the sun," was credited with miraculous powers. Not only could it help transmute base metals into gold, it reputedly could soften glass, render its owner invisible at will, or give an alchemist the ability to levitate. Some people believed that the stone would enable them to converse with angels or even to understand the language of animals.

One way the philosophers' stone could produce invisibility was by creating a "mist of heaven" which would envelop the holder and render him invisible to all around him. However, a philosophers' stone is really not needed in order to produce a "mist of invisibility." Adepts have known for a long time that with the right mental attitude, and a little practice, a supernatural mist can be formed in order to render a person invisible from prying eyes.

INVISIBILITY AND LEVITATION

STEPS TO FORMING YOUR OWN MIST

Steve Richards in his book, *Invisibility* (Aquarian Press), states that the reader should consider themselves alchemists with their own laboratories. The laboratory in this case is mostly atmosphere. What is needed is a room with limited light coming in from the outside. One bare wall is also essential, or perhaps a door that leads into a darkened room. Most important of all is privacy. A skeptic in the room will insure failure. The methods are simple, you just need to have patience and take the time.

Sit quietly and comfortably. You should then direct your gaze to one single area. This is important. The cloud will then form at the place that holds your attention. If you shift your gaze to other spots in the room, the cloud will not have a chance to build up. Your effort is cumulative. The longer you look at one area, the more definite the cloud becomes.

For best results Richards suggest you defocus your eyes. Look beyond what is in front of you, as if you are looking ten miles away. Some authorities suggest that you keep your eyes half closed. With this idea you will have to experiment. Some experts say a cloud forms better against a black background rather than a white one. You will have to practice de-focusing your eyes. With a little concentration you can do it. Without it, the technique is useless.

Chanting is suggested, but it can be distracting. Richards does not recommend it for that reason. Remember, you have to stare, de-focus your eyes, and then chant. That could be asking for too much. Again, if you don't have absolute privacy, forget it. If you feel that you must chant to help you form the cloud, use the mantra RA-MA, which is the name of a Hindu god and the name of a city where the School of Prophets

28

was founded in ancient Palestine. RA represents the masculine energy. MA is the negative, feminine potency. Together, they are the creative power that brought the universe into existence out of the cloud in the beginning. Draw out each syllable and repeat them twenty or twenty-five times per session. If it works for you, fine. If you get no results, drop it.

Another good chanting method is to chant the vowel sounds, A, E, I, O, U. Chant each sound slowly so you can feel each resonating through different parts of the body. Each vowel will effect a different place in your body. Do this for about ten minutes, don't forget to breath deeply with sound, don't hold your breath, just breath deeply and then let it out with each vowel sound.

Patience is the secret key here. Don't be discouraged. It won't happen that you will see a cloud for the first time; it may not happen after scores of times. However, it will happen if you stick with it.

What you may see after some good efforts is something that looks like heat waves. That shows that you are heading in the right direction. With practice, the waves will start to solidify, becoming more and more dense and taking on the appearance of a slight fog or mist.

If your backdrop is white, you may assume you are getting results when you see a faint blue image. This will look somewhat like the blue after image you see after someone has taken your picture with a flash bulb. One thing is certain, when you do achieve results you won't be able to see anything on the other side of the cloud.

The next step includes building the cloud. You do this by starting with your hands about a foot or so apart. Then bring them together. Think that you are compressing astral material between your hands. You bring your hands together and then separate them much like a man playing the accordion. This technique may work for you, and if it does you are likely to see balls of light between your hands. If it doesn't, try another technique.

One that you may be successful with concerns will power and eye movement. Your hands are not involved. Once the cloud has started to form, look away from it. Permit the energy to collect in another region of space. After a moment, bring your eyes gradually toward the center, where the main cloud is forming. While you are doing this, command your will power to force the energy in other parts of the room to join with the energy already in the cloud. You can glance below the cloud, and to either side of it. Above all, do not strain your eyes. It's not necessary. In fact, your eyes should be passive. All of what you do must be with your mind.

Remember to take a break when you start to feel fatigued. These techniques cannot be forced or hurried. Taking breaks helps to relieve the tedium which too often accompanies occult experimentation.

In his definitive work, Steve Richards notes that you will probably have some trouble with your cloud after it has formed. It will have a tendency to scatter to the four corners of the room. This is natural and is in accordance with the law of thermodynamics. If you allow it to happen, all the energy in the cloud will become evenly dispersed throughout the room. The action of being dispersed takes the form of a spin or vortex. To prevent that from happening, a counter spin must be produced. The dispersing spin is always in a clockwise direction. What you must do is will it to turn in a counterclockwise direction. What will happen then is that the cloud will become smaller and denser. Using this method, some experts have been able to block out the light of a 100-watt bulb. The method has also been compared with forming a nebulae in outer space. Galaxies are allegedly formed this way, with huge clouds spinning and condensing until they form stars and planets.

INVISIBILITY AND LEVITATION

One of the secrets of invisibility seems to be for
an individual to wrap themselves inside a
"cloud" or mist-like vapor. Entire armies
have been known to vanish under such conditions.

INVISIBILITY AND LEVITATION

At this point Richards says you are now ready to make yourself invisible with the help of your cloud. We will assume that you have a definite cloud with lots of astral substance in it. You must now draw the cloud around you so that you will be invisible. The cloud has to be big enough to completely cover you.

There may be a shine to the cloud. You don't want that because the shine is like a beacon. What you want is something neutral, something that will blend with your background. Use your will power for this, the shine can be suppressed with a little effort.

When the large cloud has enshrouded you, look into a mirror to see if you see your reflection. It you don't see it, you have done it!

While you are perfecting your art, you may also experiment with materializations. You might try producing lights in your room, columns of smoke, or images. You should also be able to produce spontaneous sounds such as knocks or even voices.

While talking to a friend recently, we both noticed a tendency to sometimes lose things. They just weren't where we remembered putting them. After much searching, we go back to an area we just looked, and unexpectedly, the item is suddenly there.

Rather than attributing these mysterious disappearances to elves or poltergeists, we decided it must be some kind of stress induced "negative hallucination," a condition where you are prevented from seeing something that you really need at the moment.

Mystics have told of their ability to induce a "mental confusion" in those around them. This takes two forms, one of which is a cloud or mental fog which is impressionable by another's thoughts, the other takes advantage of the brain not wanting to deal with anything that doesn't immediately fit into the person's view of reality, such as a chaotic or complex image.

When looking towards such an area, the eye will jump past the overly complex image, seeking to find familiar visual territory that doesn't require a high degree of analysis. This phenomenon has been noted with the Native Americans who could not see the first Spanish ships that were clearly visible in the harbor. Only when someone else described what they were seeing, could the rest of the group begin to see the reality. Almost like a visual hundredth monkey effect.

A Russian mentalist and paranormal researcher by the name of Vasiliev, spoke of an incident where he passed a blank piece of paper to a bank teller. The teller then gave him 1000 ruble's in return. Vasiliew said that he had projected an image into the tellers' mind that the paper was a cashiers check in the amount of 1000 rubles. The money was returned after witnesses testified to the success of the experiment.

Another experiment by Vasiliew was based on a bet with Stalin. Many of the Russian scientists had no patience with paranormal investigations, but Vasiliev and some of his colleagues wanted to establish a research institute to investigate and perfect useful techniques.

Vasiliev made a bet with Stalin that if he could appear in Stalin's private study at 8 PM on a specified weeknight, Stalin would agree to establish a research institute for paranormal investigations.

Stalin was always heavily guarded, even at home, so he thought this would be a sure bet. On the appointed night, Stalin was sitting in front of his fireplace reading, when the clock struck 8 o'clock. He heard a clearing of the throat, looked up and saw Vasiliev sitting in an armchair opposite him.

INVISIBILITY AND LEVITATION

Stalin immediately called in the guards and demanded to know how Vasiliev had gotten past all of them. Each denied they had seen Vasiliev that night. Finally, before Stalin could have them all put to death, Vasiliev explained that he had projected the image of one of Stalin's most trusted advisors into the minds of the soldiers as he walked through.

This advisor was of such high rank that he was allowed to come and go without challenge by the soldiers. It was at this point that Stalin was convinced of the usefulness of psychic research and funded the highly effective Russian paranormal research efforts.

When I was about 15 years of age, I experienced a peculiar event that left a lasting impression. We had a local newsstand that received new magazines and paperback books once a week. Being a heavy reader, I had a friend who I often met there as we went through looking for books and magazines on UFOs, paranormal, and science fiction.

One night, we were to meet at 7 PM. I arrived first and climbed onto a ladder with my feet about 2 feet off the floor so that I was easy to spot from anywhere in this small shop. This shop also had only one door with an aisle having books and magazines on each side of the aisle. I heard someone enter, turned around and it was my friend. He looked around the shop, apparently without seeing me. What made this so strange was that I was right in front of him, no more then ten feet away.

I was puzzled about this, thinking he had not said hello because he must be kidding around. Prior to his entry, I was very absorbed in a new paperback book that I was contemplating buying. A few minutes later, I stepped off the ladder and walked up to him.

INVISIBILITY AND LEVITATION

My friend was startled and asked how I'd gotten into the shop without passing by him. I explained that I'd been there all along. He thought I was lying and asked the cashier who confirmed I'd been there for at least 30 minutes. It was very strange. I don't know if he was distracted or if my deep concentration on the book produced some kind of "cloud of confusion" to his perception of the surroundings.

What is the purpose of all this? Why would the human mind need the potential to induce Invisibility. The answer could be, Invulnerability. In the past, man was vulnerable to all kinds of wild predators. In this day and age we are no longer prey to wild animals. However, new dangers face us every day. We can be potential victims of muggers, killers, speeding vehicles, and other modern-day dangers. To be invisible is to be invulnerable. You are able to isolate yourself from whatever danger is present.

INVISIBILITY AND THE ART OF INVULNERABILITY

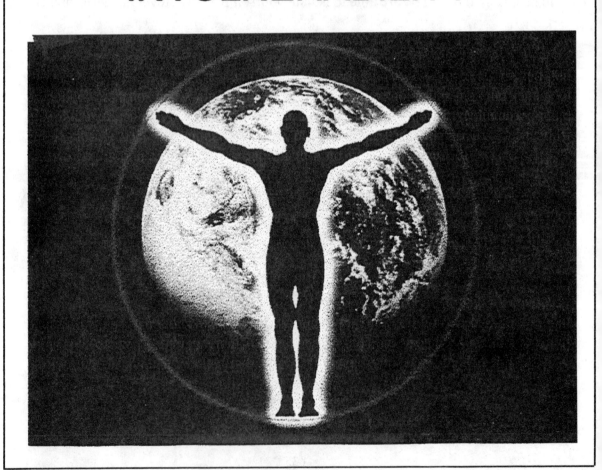

INVISIBILITY AND LEVITATION

Madame Blavatsky on Invulnerability

"The astral fluid can be compressed about a person so as to form an elastic shell, absolutely non-penetrable by any physical object, however great the velocity with which it travels. In a word, this fluid can be made to equal and even excel in resisting power, water and air.

"In India, Malabar, and some places of Central Africa, the conjurers will freely permit any traveler to fire his musket or revolver at them, without touching the weapon themselves or selecting the balls. In Laing's *'Travels Among the Timanni, the Kourankos, and the Soulimas,'* occurs a description by an English traveler, the first white man to visit the tribe of the Soulimas, of a very curious scene. A body of picked soldiers fired upon a chief who had nothing to defend himself with but certain talismans. Although their muskets were properly loaded and aimed, not a ball could strike him. Salverte gives a similar case in the *Philosophy of Occult Sciences*: 'In 1568 the Prince of Orange condemned a Spanish prisoner to be shot at Juliers; the soldiers tied him to a tree and fired, but he was invulnerable. They at last stripped him to see what armor he wore, but found only an amulet. When this was taken from him, he fell dead at the first shot.'

"Many travelers, this writer included, have witnessed instances of this invulnerability where deception was impossible. A few years ago, there lived in a African village an Abyssinian, who passed for a sorcerer. Upon on occasion a party of Europeans, going to Sudan, amused themselves for an hour or two in firing at him with their own pistols and muskets, a privilege which he gave them for a trifling fee. As many as five shots were fired simultaneously, and the muzzles of the pieces were not above two yards distant from the sorcerer's breast.

"In each case, simultaneously with the flash, the bullet would appear just behind the muzzle, quivering in the air, and then fall harmlessly to the ground. A German offered the magician a five franc piece if he would allow him to fire the gun with the muzzle touching his body. The magician at first refused, but finally, after appearing to hold a conversation with someone inside the ground, consented. The experimenter carefully loaded, and pressing the muzzle of the weapon against the sorcerer's body, fired. The barrel burst into fragments as far down as the stock, and the magician walked off unhurt.

"In our own time several well-known mediums have frequently, in the presence of the most respectable witnesses, not only handled blazing coals and actually placed their faces upon a fire without singeing a hair, but even laid flaming coals upon the hands and heads of bystanders. The well-known story of the Indian chief, who confessed to General George Washington that at Braddock's defeat he fired his rifle at him seventeen times without effect, will recur to the reader in this connection."

Obviously, all of the invulnerable people mentioned by Madame Blavatsky were protected by a cloud made up of astral material, or ectoplasm. It was invisible to the naked eye, but quite strong, strong enough to stop a bullet. However, this is one experiment we would advise you not to try no matter how strong you think your own cloud is.

HOW TO ACHIEVE CLOUDLESS INVISIBILITY

Madame David-Neel explained in her book, *Magic and Mystery in Tibet*, that if you walk among crowds shouting and bumping into people you will make yourself quite visible. But, if you walk noiselessly, touching no one, looking at no one, you may be able to pass without being seen. Animals do this all the time to catch prey. It has also been pointed out that if you sit motionless you can cut down on your visibility.

INVISIBILITY AND LEVITATION

However there is a drawback to this method. Your mind generates disquiteness. David-Neel says, "The work of the mind generates an energy which spreads all around the one who produces it, and this energy is felt in various ways by those who come into touch with it. The idea is to cut off that source of energy, or noise. If you can do that you become as silent as anyone can be. You may still be seen. That is, a camera or mirror would pick up your image, but you would not be noticed.

Said one expert: "When the mind inhibits emanation of its radioactivity it ceases to be the source of mental stimuli to others, so that they become unconscious of the presence of an Adept of the Art, just as they are unconscious of invisible beings living in a rate of vibration unlike their own."

Aleister Crowley wrote: "The real secret of invisibility is not concerned with the laws of optics at all. The trick is to prevent people noticing you when they would normally do so."

Apparently, Crowley had the power to keep people from noticing him. In an experiment, he took a walk along a street dressed in a golden crown and a scarlet robe. He did not attract attention to himself.

Eliphas Levi points out: "A man, for example, pursued by murderers, after having run down a side street, returns instantly and comes, with a calm face, toward those who are pursuing him, or mixes with them and appears occupied with the same pursuit. He will certainly render himself invisible. The person who would be seen is always remarked, and he who would remain unnoticed effaces himself and disappears."

In 1925 Marie Harlowe had a strange experience that convinced her in the reality of invisibility. At that time she worked in a small western town in an industrial office. After a disagreement with a local jeweler over the cost of a ring, Harlowe had to hurriedly catch a train to keep an appointment in a nearby town.

After she had got on the train she noticed the conductor, the jeweler and the local sheriff enter the car she was seated in. All three men came down the aisle and stopped directly where she was sitting. The conductor said, "She was sitting right here. I don't know if she got off or not, but here is where she was sitting."

The conductor was anxious to get the train going, and the other two men got off the train, mumbling about looking for her in the train station. While the men were close to Harlowe in the train aisle, the conductor stood on her foot, leaving a dirty smudge on her white shoe.

At that point Harlowe realized that she had been invisible to the three men and a half-full train car of passengers. Thinking back, she knew immediately on seeing the jeweler and the sheriff that she was going to be arrested. She felt that time stood still as she desired to be invisible more than anything else she had ever wanted.

The train started up, and the conductor was a very surprised man when he saw Harlowe sitting where he had last seen her. Afterwards, the jeweler dropped the charges against her, admitting that he had been trying to swindle her out of some extra money.

Since that involuntary experience of making her physical body invisible, Marie Harlowe learned a great deal about the conscious method of producing this phenomena. A Hindu student suggested that she had not really dematerialized on the train and became invisible, but had only hypnotized the three men.

Harlowe speculated that due to her Yoga excercises, particularly methods of

INVISIBILITY AND LEVITATION

breathing, that she had developed a **Will** as related to bodily and mental functions, which is needed for a person to produce phenomena of this type.

Tibetan Tantra Yoga teaches much, and in detail, about the art of invisibility. It declares that it is a matter of shape-shifting of the bodily form. Through direction of a subtle mental faculty or psychic power, whereby all forms, animate and inanimate, including man's own form, are created, the human body can either be dissolved, and thereby made invisible, by magically inhibiting the faculty, or be mentally imperceptible to others, and thus equally invisible to them by changing the body's vibration.

The mind can inhibit emanation of its radioactivity, and thus cease to be mental stimuli to others, so they become unconscious of the presence of that person. We are always unconscious of many invisible beings living in different vibratory expressions than our own.

The process according to Evans-Wents, who wrote and translated several books on Tibetan Tantra Yoga, is "giving palpable being to visualization," as an architect makes his two-dimension plans three dimensional, but in reverse.

In the experience on the train, Harlowe did not "go" anywhere. She was there all the time, conscious of everything going on, evidenced by the mark made on her shoe. She had simply drawn the shutters. (Changed the body rate of vibrations).

Those wishing to learn the secret art of invisiblity ought to study a little of Tantric Yoga. Madame David-Neel, by these methods, produced a "living" form which stayed with her day and night, in sight of those around her. However, it took her six months of psychic struggle to get the form disolved.

41

INVISIBILITY AND LEVITATION

All of which makes more understandable the story of the Japanese man who meditated upon creating himself as a butterfly form, and thereafter was never sure that he was a man who thought he had been a butterfly, or a butterfly who now thought he was a man.

A SIMPLE METHOD

Sit quietly. Close your eyes. Allow your consciousness to slowly turn inward. Believe it or not, this does not require any effort. It's a natural and involuntary process. The first step is to blot out your environment. Make yourself oblivious to it. Next, keep in your mind the thought that you want to hide. Do this even though you may be sitting in an open room with other people around. Finally, eliminate all thoughts from your mind. This is probably the hardest thing for most people to accomplish, emptying all thoughts from your mind. Most of us find that our minds are almost always working. When we attempt to clear our heads, thoughts and images flood in at a fantastic rate.

To try and clean your mind of intruding thoughts, try concentrating on one particular thing. If you are of a religious mind, try the image of Jesus. Others have reported success with visualizing a clear, white light. While others like to form a pentagram with their mind. Whatever your choice, remember, the goal is to remove all thought from your mind.

Remember, thoughts produce energy, and energy makes you more visible. Stop thinking, remain motionless with eyes closed, and you become invisible. Not in the literal sense of the word, but unnoticed.

J.H. Brennan has devised a method to stop thought-energy. He says that if he cannot stop himself from shouting, he can conceal himself from you by surrounding himself with a soundproof screen that shuts out the noise. He uses the word "shouting" to mean "thinking." There is a technique for doing that and it is taught by the AMORC Rosicrucians.

THE VEIL OF OBSCURITY

With this technique you can actually produce real invisibility. The Rosicrucians advise you to sit quietly as though you are meditating. Close your eyes. Now imagine that you are completely surrounded by a soundproof screen. Think of it as a curtain hanging down all around you, completely concealing you. Think of the curtain until you can feel its presence, keeping in mind that the curtain will make you invisible to others.

How can you tell if your experiment is successful? Simple. Place a mirror at the opposite side of the room, beyond the Veil's influence. You will be able to see through the curtain, but outsiders will not be able to see in. If you are successful, you will not see your image in the mirror.

However, don't hope for success immediately. Give yourself plenty of time to achieve it. Be patient, and never become discouraged. Acquiring occult powers is not easy. You can be sure that those who are successful are those who have enormous patience.

THE INANIMATE-ANIMATE ASSUMPTION METHOD

This is an amazing psychic experiment that can get you inside of objects, animals or people for brand new sensations. It is a form of being invisible, but not quite in the sense that you have so far mastered. This is object control and mind control. If done successfully, you can find out things about objects and people that will be nothing short of incredible.

The beginner should start with an object that is made up of a single material. A piece of steel or copper is good, so is a crystal or a small piece of wood.

With the object in front of you, close your eyes and sit quietly. Visualize the object in your mind's eye. While you do that, enlarge the object. Think of it as growing, gradually, into something as large as, say, a door. Then think of yourself as moving into the object, merging with it, so that you are invisible to others inside this huge piece of steel or copper.

Now you are psychically one with the object. What do you do now? Keep you senses alive. Find out what you can see, feel, hear, smell. Is it cold or warm inside? What sensations do you feel?

The answers to these questions won't come immediately. They will, however, emerge after you have succeeded with the method several times. This is another instance when your initial failures should be overlooked. The stance to take is: if others have done it, so can I.

The next step in the assumption method is to use a plant or a tree. If no trees are available to you, try a leaf on a house plant. You may pick a leaf and bring it into your house, but this represents a problem. A picked leaf is a dying one. There is still some life force in it, but it is waning.

INVISIBILITY AND LEVITATION

It's best to try the experiment on a plant that is totally alive and still growing. Repeat the experiment that you performed with the inanimate object. Visualize the plant becoming extremely large. Use your imagination and see yourself merging with it. Check out your sensations while merged with the plant. When you have conquered that part of the method, move on to animals and humans.

Getting an animal or a human to sit for you while you assume to merge may be a problem, but at this stage of the game you are proficient enough to visualize the entity without having the physical presence. You are going to visualize the person anyway with your eyes closed, so you merely have to visualize that he or she is standing before you.

Merging with another person psychically is somewhat tricky. You are going to assume a merger, and for best results that individual should have his back to you in your imagination. Visualize putting your hands on both sides of his head. In your mind's eye, think and see yourself removing his head and putting it over your own head.

With his head on your shoulders, try to see with his eyes, hear with his ears, think with his brain. Yours and his thoughts should merge. There now should be telepathic communications, with you planting thoughts into his brain without his
being aware of where they came from.

In the beginning of this phase of your experiment you may get only slight impressions from you host. You may see something that will tell you where he is at the moment of your assumption. In all likelihood you will have nothing. But stay with it. Practice will make you a success.

Here are some examples of others who have mastered this technique:

INVISIBILITY AND LEVITATION

- College students have merged with their professors to find out what questions they intended to ask on examinations.

- People who work with machinery have merged with the machinery to find out what was wrong.

- Computer technicians who have mastered the assumption method have merged with their computers to locate the bugs in the devices - - - an advantage that saved them scores of man-hours in their work.

- Veterinarians who are unable to diagnose an illness in an animal by normal means will enter the pets mind to discover what the problem is.

- Gardeners can merge with their flowers and vegetables to ensure a perfect crop.

PRAYERS
AND
SPELLS FOR
INVISIBILITY

INVISIBILITY AND LEVITATION

Some people who practice invisibility find that it helps to do some conjuring to get them into the mood. This is not true of those who follow the path of Yoga. You can be highly religious or an atheist, it makes no difference at all. But with magic, faith is required. It does not matter which faith you follow, but if you are going to invocate or pray, you should believe in the Supreme Deity or else you are being hypocritical.

This is the first prayer:

"Scaeboles, Arbaron, Elohi, Elimigith, Herenobulcule, Methe, Timayal, Villaquiel, Teveni, Yevie, Ferete, Bacuhavba, Guvarin; through Him through Whom ye have empire and power over men, ye must accomplish this work so that I may go and remain invisible.

"O thou Almiras, Master of Invisibility, with thy Ministers Cheros, Maitor, Tangedem, Transidium, Suvantos, Abelaios, Bored, Belamith, Castumi, Dabuel; I conjure ye by Him who maketh Earth and Heaven to tremble, Who is seated upon the throne of His majesty, that this operation may be perfectly accomplished according to my will, so that at whatsoever time it may please me, I may be able to be invisible."

When you have said that prayer you may want to say another to help you conjure up the cloud that will make you invisible.

"Come to me, O shroud of darkness and of night, by the power of the name Yeheshuah, Yehovashah. Formulate about me, thou divine egg of the darkness of spirit. I conjure ye, O particles of astral darkness, that ye enfold me as a guard and shroud of utter silence and mystery.

"I conjure and invoke this shroud of concealment. I invoke ye and conjure ye. I

48

evoke ye potently. I command and constrain ye. I compel ye to absolute, instant, and complete obedience, and that without deception and delay. And I declare that with the divine Aid in this Operation I shall succeed, that the shroud shall conceal me alike from men and spirits, that it shall be under my control, ready to disperse and to re-form at my command."

Another prayer in the form of a verse:

"Gather, ye flakes of Astral light
To shroud my form in your substantial Night;
Clothe me, and hide me, but at my control,
Darken men's eyes, and blind their souls;
Gather, O gather, at my word divine,
For ye are the Watchers, my soul is the shrine."

Still another prayer which may help you achieve your success:

"O ye strong and mighty ones of the Sphere of Shabbathai, ye Aralim, I conjure ye by the mighty name of Yhvh Elohim, the divine ruler of Binah, and by the name of Tzaphqiel, your Archangel. Aid me with your power, in your office to place a veil between me and all things belonging to the outer and material world. Clothe me with a veil woven from that silent darkness which surrounds your abode of eternal rest in the Sphere of Shabbathai."

When the moment comes that you want to become visible again, you may say the following prayer:

"In the name of Yhvh Elohim, I invoke thee, who art clothed with the Sun, who

INVISIBILITY AND LEVITATION

standest upon the Moon, and art crowned with the crown of twelve stars. Aima Elohim, Shekinah, Who art Darkness illuminated by the Light divine, send me thine Archangel Tzaphqiel, and thy legions of Aralim, the mighty angels of the Sphere of Shabbathai, that I may disintegrate and scatter this shroud of darkness and of mystery, for its work is ended for the hour.

"I conjure Thee, O shroud of darkness and of Mystery, which has well served my purpose, that thou now depart unto thine ancient ways. But be ye, whether by word or will, or by this great invocation of your powers, ready to come quickly and forcibly to my behest, again to shroud me from the eyes of men. And now I say unto ye, depart in peace, with the blessing of God the Vast and Shrouded One, and be ye very ready to come when ye are called."

These conjurations may help you to concentrate; and they may not. If they distract you, then they won't work for you. In any event, they are here for your benefit if you need something extra to aid you in becoming invisible.

An interesting spell for invisibility was written up in *The Circle Network News* Winter 93/94, Vol.15: Number 4 by author: Mara Ravensong Bluewater. The spell is a tried and true recipe for an invisibility manifesting preparation. The spell is presented as a powder, to be strewn, burned, or carried, the herbs given could just as well be concocted into a potion, oil, or tincture.

Invisibility Powder

At Dark Moon, in a mortar and pestle, grind together:

1 part Fern leaf, dried

INVISIBILITY AND LEVITATION

1 part Poppy seeds

Add:

2 parts Slippery Elm powder
1 part Myrrh
1 part Marjoram, dried
3 parts Dillweed, fresh if possible

Grind all together, mixing well.

Add 9 drops almond tincture (almond cooking extract is great.) with enough spring water to make everything barely moist, and mix in well.

Place in a ceramic bowl, spreading as thinly as possible, and dry the mixture over low heat, stirring it occasionally, until it seems lightly browned. Pour back into mortar, and grind again, enchanting:

Things Seen, and Things Not Seen:
Let me walk here in between.

When finely powdered, store in a clear glass container. It will keep its power for years. Sprinkle, just a little bit, on yourself, objects, or in a place to be made invisible.

Another old herbal method of inducing invisibility involved using the poisonous Christmas rose. The plant was believed to serve in numerous powerful spells, including one that could ensure invisibility.

INVISIBILITY AND LEVITATION

On the night of the new moon those wishing to become invisible must first bath themselves with rose water. Afterwards you must sit quietly and envision yourself to be as dark as the night of the new moon. At least 15 minutes of this mental activity must take place before any attempt at invisibility is made.

At this point you must take the Christmas rose and tear it apart. As you take the plant apart, say with each piece, "these are my feet, these are my legs, this is my torso, these are my arms, these are my shoulders, this is my head."

After completely tearing the plant into ten pieces then say out loud to the open sky: "As each piece of this plant disappears into the dark of the new moon, so will each piece of my body. With that, throw each piece, one at a time into the darkness. At the end of the ritual your body should be as dark as the night. As long as you do not make loud noises or attempt to draw unnecessary attention to yourself. You will remain unseen until the first light of the morning.

Another spell that has been handed down over the years involves taking a long cloak or coat and dipping it into the water of a pure running stream. You must do this everyday for twenty-eight days, starting on the first day of the new moon, and ending on the last day of the full moon.

You have to dip the coat thirteen times each day in order for the spell to work. On the beginning of the new month you can then wear the coat becoming as clear as the pure water. Unfortunately in modern times this spell probably won't work. The reason being is the difficulty finding a pure running stream of natural water. Any kind of pollution will negate the spell. Nor can you use filtered water, it must be clean, pure, natural water or the spell will not work.

PROOF EXISTS FOR THE REALITY OF INVISIBILITY

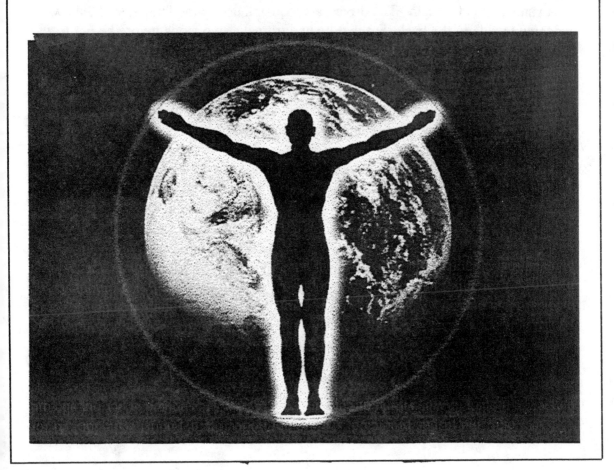

INVISIBILITY AND LEVITATION

We've talked about how to become invisible, and we have dealt with the masters who know how to do it, but your must be asking yourself by now if the art is impossible. No one does it in real life. You have never come in contact with invisibility, nor do you know of anyone who has. Maybe so, but you can't convince Ernest Poindexter and Meredith Wright that they did not come in contact with an invisible man.

The date was September 1963 in Seattle, Washington. Ernest and Meredith at that time were nine years old. On that Saturday morning they were hitchhiking their way downtown to go to the movies.

A van stopped for them. The driver, an acquaintance of the family, said they were welcome to ride in the back, but that he had to make two stops before he got to the downtown area. Ernest and Meredith climbed in the back amid packages.

A few minutes later the driver stopped at a store where he had to make a delivery. He set the hand brake and put the transmission into reverse gear because he was parked on a hill.

While the driver was in the store, another vehicle pulled in behind the van and bumped it accidentally. The van started to roll. The hill was steep, and in no time at all the van was rolling at break-neck speed. Some parked cars were dead ahead. The children were panic-stricken. They didn't know what to do. There would be a terrible collision in a few seconds and there was nothing they could do about it.

Suddenly, the van lurched to the left and avoided the parked cars. A voice yelled out, "Don't be scared boys, just hang on tight. I'm going to apply the brakes."

INVISIBILITY AND LEVITATION

The voice appeared to be coming from the drivers seat, but no one was there. Their eyes were glued to the steering wheel because it was turning by itself. Then the horn blew. They could see it being depressed as if by an unseen hand. Pedestrians scampered out of the way.

Finally, at the bottom of the hill the van rolled to a stop. People came running over. The boys climbed down to the street. The van's driver hurried over to them. He said, "If you boys hadn't steered that truck you could have been killed."

Ernest said, "But we didn't steer it."

A pedestrian confirmed the boy's statement, saying that he saw the van and that no one was behind the wheel. Another onlooker said he saw the boys in the back, sitting on cartons, and that they were not behind the wheel.

The final confirmation came when the horn suddenly blew by itself in front of the astonished crowd. The two boys raced off. They wanted no part of the invisible man who came to their rescue.

Now that we know that invisibility does exist, it is not difficult to understand that at least one person in the Seattle area had accomplished the feat and had put it to good use.

HOW INVISIBILITY GAINED A KINGDOM

A shepherd named Gyges was caught in a violent storm while tending his flock. Then an earthquake ripped the ground asunder near where he was sitting. Gyges peered into the gap in the earth and saw to his surprise that it contained a hollow brazen horse. There were doors on each side of the horse. Gyges scampered down into the crevasse and opened one of the doors. Inside was an extremely large man who was obviously dead. He was nude except for a golden ring. Being a resourceful young man, Gyges took the ring and put it on his own finger.

This story, which comes from the works of Plato, continued with Gyges meeting with other shepherds during their monthly get-together. Their job was to prepare a report for the king concerning the state of their flocks. Gyges chatted away with his friends and played with the golden ring on his finger. He noticed that when he turned it so that the collet was inside his hand, the others in the group spoke of him as though he was no longer present. He realized in astonishment that the ring could make him invisible as long as he turned the collet to the inside of his hand.

Gyges saw great possibilities with the ring. He managed to get himself on the committee that was to present the monthly report to the king. Once inside the palace, he made himself invisible and hurried to the queen's chambers. He made love to the queen, who decided on the spot that Gyges was a better lover than the king. They then conspired to kill the king, which they did. And Gyges became the king of Lydia.

Plato let the story end there, but added a moral which said in essence to never trust an invisible man. Plato wrote: "Suppose that there were two such magic rings, and the just (man) put on one of them and the unjust man the other. No man can be imagined to be of such an iron nature that he would stand fast in justice. No man would keep his hands off what was not his own when he could safely take what he liked out of the market, or go into house and lie with anyone at his pleasure, or kill or release from prison whom he would, and in all respects be like a god among men.

"If you could imagine anyone obtaining this power of becoming invisible, and never doing any wrong or touching what was another's, he would be thought by the lookers-on to be a most wretched idiot. Although they would praise him to one another's faces, and keep up appearances with one another from fear that they, too, might suffer in injustice."

Plato was quite astute, although he did overlook the certainty, as one sage put it, "that God doth see both them and their knavery." Still, the philosopher's point is well taken. There is an ethical problem with invisibility, moreso if one came upon a magic ring that could do the job. Fortunately, magic rings are few and far between.

A Chinese alchemist was wary of invisibility, saying that the techniques "are not to be used heedlessly, such as for example to produce outbursts of amazement when employed without reason in company. They may be used only in dire necessity against military reversals and dangerous crises, for in that way no harm will be incurred."

The Arab mystics and alchemists agree. They insist that invisibility should be used only on the battlefield and during a reversal of fortune. We must remember that these are ancient beliefs and that in today's world one cannot become invisible if one has an evil intent. That should have been clear even four centuries ago when two Spaniards wanted to kill the Prince of Orange. They assumed that they could do something similar to what Gyges did to gain the kingdom. The method they used has been lost, but we do know that apparently only one of them could become invisible, and only if he took all of his clothes off.

The date was March 18, 1582. The Spaniard who agreed to make himself invisible failed to look into a mirror to see if the experiment was successful. Instead, he walked naked to the palace. A guard let him pass. The Spaniard thought he was truly invisible because the guard gave no hint that he saw him. Actually he kept the naked man in view at all times, and when it appeared that the odd-looking stranger was intent on harming the prince, he was stopped. For his effort, the Spaniard was flogged soundly.

INVISIBILITY AND LEVITATION

THE RING OF GYGES

Tradition has handed down through the ages the method of making the Ring of Gyges. For most however, to do so would mean Herculean feats of legerdemain.

The first step says to use fixed mercury. This is an alchemical term, and that refers to the Mercury of the Wise. Simply put, the Mercury of the Wise is the material that goes into the cloud you conjure up to make yourself invisible. Would it be even possible to shape this ethereal material into a solid ring?

The next step is even more difficult: You are to engrave the words "Jesus, passant par le milieu d'eux s'en allait" on the ring. The translation is that Jesus made himself invisible when he walked among the Pharisees. We are not told how to engrave something on a cloud.

The ring must be set with a small stone found in the lapwing's nest. This is called Quiritia. Finding a lapwing bird may not be easy.

There are also certain mystifications that come from the rather vulgar grimoires. Since we are not likely to make such a ring, why bother? There are other ridiculous methods of becoming invisible, such as weaving the hairs from the head of a hyena. Those hairs are so short that it would be close to impossible to weave them.

We think our methods of making yourself invisible are much more sensible, however you should be aware of the more far-fetched methods as they may well have worked for someone else in the past.

INVISIBILITY AND LEVITATION

THE STRANGE CASE OF MADAME BLAVATSKY

Madame Blavatsky was a Russian occultist who was said to have codified secret traditional truths into two basic textbooks, *Isis Unveiled*, and *The Secret Doctrine*. She established the Theosophical Society in 1875 with a membership of 15. Today there are 1500 branches throughout the world, with several hundred thousand members. Madame Blavatsky said that she was guided into setting up the society by a spirit, and that her acute psychic powers came from an invisible band of Tibetan "masters of wisdom."

Madame Blavatsky also claimed she had the power of invisibility. A man called Colonel Olcott wrote an eyewitness account of one incident which indicates that the woman was truly capable of this feat. Olcott wrote:

"Her house in Philadelphia was built on the local plan, with a front building and a wing at the back which contained the dining-room below and sitting or bedroom above. Madame Blavatsky's bedroom was the front room on the first floor of the main building; at the turn of the staircase was the sitting room, and from its open door one could look straight along the passage into her room if the door was open. Madame Blavatsky had been sitting in the former apartment conversing with me, but left to get something from her bedroom. I saw her mount the few steps to her floor, enter her room, and leave the door open. Time passed, but she did not return. I waited, and waited. Fearing that she might have fainted, I called her name. There was no reply, so now, being a little anxious, and knowing that she could not be engaged privately, since the door had not been closed. I went in, called again, and looked under the bed. She was not there. I looked in her closet. She was not visible anywhere. She had vanished, without the chance of having walked out in the normal way, for, save the door giving upon the landing, there was no other means of exit; the room was a cul de sac.

INVISIBILITY AND LEVITATION

"I was a cool one about phenomena after my long course of experiences, but this puzzled and worried me. I went back to the sitting room, lit a pipe, and tried to puzzle out the mystery. This was in 1875, many years before the Salpetriere school's experiments in hypnotism had been vulgarized, so it never occurred to me that I was the subject of a neat experiment in mental suggestion, and that Madame Blavatsky had simply inhibited my organs of sight from perceiving her presence, perhaps within two paces of me in the room. After a while she calmly came out of her room into the passage and returned to the sitting room to me. When I asked her where she had been, she laughed and said she had some occult business to attend to, and had made herself invisible. But how, she could not explain."

INVISIBILITY THROUGH HYPNOTISM

The subject was an 18 year old girl named Elsie B. As reported by a doctor named Binet, the servant girl was placed in a deep hypnotic trance. The hypnotist told her: "When you awaken you will no longer see me. I shall have gone."

She woke, and just as predicted, she did not notice the hypnotist. She looked for him, even though he was sitting directly in front of her. He shouted at her but she did not hear him. He stuck pins into her flesh, but she did not feel the pain. "As far as she was concerned," the hypnotist said, "I had ceased to exist, and all the acoustic, visual, tactile, and other impressions emanating from myself did not make the slightest impression upon her; she ignored them all . . . Wishing to see, on account of its medical-legal bearing, whether a serious offense might be committed under cover of hypnosis, I roughly raised her dress and skirt. Although naturally very modest, she allowed this without a blush. A moment later, though, she was blushing a very great deal."

That was because the hypnotist suggested to her that she would remember that incidents that, a moment before, she did not even seem to be aware of. She did remember, yet she was altogether unable to believe that she had allowed herself to be exposed, and, when queried, reported that she remembered the incident as if it took place in a dream.

The demonstration harkens back to ancient times when people were struck blind without any apparent damage to the eyes. Today the condition is called hysteria or conversion neurosis, and people are rarely "struck blind" because faith is the essential factor in the disease, and faith is the essential factor in the cure.

Peter B.C. Fenwick a London psychiatrist and neurophysiologist, conducted research on a woman known as Ruth because of her ability to see apparitions that looked as real to her as living persons did. These apparitions did not have the insubstantial quality of ghosts or dreams. Ruth said they obstructed her view of things just as real people would.

Fenwick fitted Ruth with electrodes on her scalp. The electrodes showed through an oscilloscope, that electrical waves from the vision center of Ruth's brain were stimulated every time she created one of her apparitions. To Ruth's brain, her mind created apparitions that were as real as the electrodes on her head.

When asked how did she make an apparition, Ruth replied: "I stop paying attention to everything around me. I decide whose apparition I want to make. I remember what the person looks like, as most people do with their eyes closed, except my eyes are open. And I produce the person."

Tests showed that when Ruth was seeing and hearing an apparition, her brain reacted as it would when perceiving a live person. Ruth's ability shows that the brain can be instructed to "see" what is not there, and to "not see" what is there.

INVISIBILITY AND LEVITATION

With the proper types of practice, a person can influence the minds of those around him to literally "not see" you. This is why learning to control your own thoughts is so important. In order to control the minds of those you want to be invisible to, you must be able to control your own mind. A noisy, energetic mind will allow your image to "bleed" over into other minds. As long as your image remains in the brains of those you are trying to disappear from, invisibility will be impossible.

SPONTANEOUS INVISIBILITY

Researcher Donna Higbee is a hypnotherapist in Santa Barbara, California. Higbee runs a support group for people who believe that they have experienced some form of encounter and/or abduction by alien entities. The meetings offer a totally open and safe space for a dialogue regarding personal experiences, personal beliefs, and the implications of what such encounters might mean in a larger sense for this planet.

Donna was not surprised when a woman asked to speak about something that she didn't know how to deal with or understand. After hearing the story, Higbee at first thought there was the possibility that this individual was highly imaginative. However, when a second person some time later spoke of the same thing, Donna Higbee decided to look into the situation further.

Vera (pseudonym), the first woman, had a very unusual story: Vera had driven her car to the post office to get stamps. She walked in and joined the line, taking the end position. Soon thereafter a man walked in and asked the man directly in front of Vera if this was the end of the line. The man ahead of Vera answered that he was indeed the end of the line, wherein Vera spoke up and said she was the end of the line. No one looked at Vera or acknowledged that she had spoken and. in fact she was almost stepped on as the second man took up the end position in line.

INVISIBILITY AND LEVITATION

Vera thought to herself how rude these people were and moved slightly to the side of the line, so as not to be jostled; she continued moving up with other people. When her time came to go to the counter to be helped, she walked up and stated her business and quite to her amazement, the man behind her walked right up and did the same. The postal clerk never acknowledged Vera but began assisting the man. Vera announced loudly that she was there first, but no one paid the slightest attention to her.

Getting very upset by this time with what she considered extreme rudeness, she just walked out of the post office and went home. A number of days later, she was attempting to get some assistance in a store and no one would help her or even acknowledge that she was present. It seemed as if she was invisible to people around her and also couldn't be heard when she spoke. She had no idea what was happening, but she certainly wasn't pleased about it.

When a second person came to Higbee with a story that seemed to involve invisibility, she began to take this a little more seriously. In brief, this woman was sitting on the sofa, letting her mind wander as she stared at the wall. The wall seemed to take on a less- than- solid form and she was fascinated with it. When she finally came out of her reverie, she was astonished to find her husband searching the house for her and she certainly had not been there. Again, although she was physically present, the woman seemed to be unseen by another person. She had become invisible.

At his point, Higbee decided to check with a number of other researchers and see if anyone else had ever heard of such a report. She was surprised to find that a number of other researchers had in just the past year or so either heard of this, or knew someone directly who had experienced something akin to spontaneous invisibility.

In every case Higbee researched, the person was physically still present, although unable to be seen or heard. From the point of view of the invisible person, the world looks normal and they have no idea that they cannot be seen or heard by people around them.

Donna Higbee spoke with two individuals in different towns in Texas who reported invisibility experiences. One woman went through a cafeteria line and when she approached the cashier, the cashier couldn't see her. It was only when the woman began to get upset that the cashier suddenly saw her standing there.

Another woman who had similar experiences wanted to conduct a little experiment. After having been ignored at a movie theater ticket window, she proceeded to walk in and out of the theater past the ticket person several times. No one ever indicated that they could see her. Then to be absolutely certain, she entered the lobby of the men's room to see if she could get stares. No one even looked her way.

Jean in Tucson, Arizona, wrote Higbee of her experiences. She has had them occur in the library when she attempted to check out books and in clothing stores. "I've had this happen in stores, in restaurants, and many places. I remember joking to a friend of mine one time that I felt like I could walk into a bank, help myself to a pile of bills and no one would ever see me because I was invisible. There is no physical reason why I should be. I'm taller than average for my sex and age group (I'm fifty-five years old and 5'9"), referred to as good-looking, and I've always worn my hair red. You wouldn't think a tall woman with red hair, high heels in a purple dress and dangle earrings would be invisible, would you?"

Then there is the story from thirty-seven year old Peter in Gloucestershire, England, who was at a private party in 1987. He walked upstairs to use the bathroom and was followed by a woman who also wanted to use the bathroom. The woman motioned for him to go first and she stood outside the door to wait her turn.

INVISIBILITY AND LEVITATION

Peter used the bathroom, opened the door and walked out into the hallway, closing the door behind him. He went on down the stairs and walked over to some friends and started talking to them. They all ignored him completely. He though they were playing a joke on him, so he walked away and found his girlfriend and asked her for a cigarette. She, too, acted like she didn't see or hear him.

Peter was getting angry by this time and thought the joke had gone too far. He decided to walk back upstairs and catch the woman coming out of the bathroom and ask her for a cigarette. "...I walked back up the stairs and, on reaching the bathroom landing, I came across the girl again who was standing outside the bathroom door, clearly still waiting for me to come out. When she saw me, her face dropped in surprise for clearly she thought that I was still in the bathroom." Peter returned to the party downstairs and everything was normal again and he was able to be seen and heard. When he questioned his friends and girlfriend as to why they had ignored him, they all swore that they had never seen or heard him. Obviously the woman upstairs had not seen him come out of the bathroom and go downstairs.

Jannise of Minneapolis, Minnesota has had a number of invisibility experiences throughout her life. As a teenager, she fell in with a group of friends who decided to see if they could actually steal something from a department store and not get caught. As luck would have it, the entire group was caught and taken into custody, including Jannise. They were taken to the police station and one by one were questioned, except for Jannise.

Although she was standing right there, no one paid the slightest attention to her; not the police, the guards, or the office personnel. She finally just got up and walked out of the police station without ever being questioned or anyone attempting to stop her. When she later talked with her friends about what happened in the police station, "...they didn't even recall me being taken into custody at the department store. Yet I rode in the police car with everyone else, and they thought I was still at the store." No one had seen her from the moment the police had arrived on the scene in the store until

65

some time after she had walked out of the police station unhindered.

Higbee wonders if there is any kind of correlation between those individuals who feel they have been aboard an alien craft, and those who are experiencing this invisibility phenomenon. It would be interesting to learn if, in passing through the force field of a craft, the abductee's own vibrational frequency is somehow altered or raised. Reported UFOs seem to have the ability to appear and disappear at will and might have a force field that alters vibrational frequency and allows for spontaneous invisibility.

EXTRATERRESTRIALS, UFOS AND HOW THEY ARE ABLE TO BECOME INVISIBLE

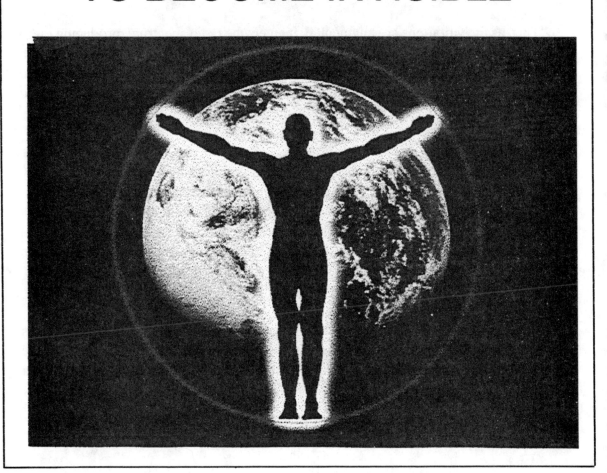

INVISIBILITY AND LEVITATION

HOW UFOs BECOME INVISIBLE

Many years ago, Alexander Graham Bell the inventor of the telephone, wrote an article for a scientific magazine explaining how it was possible for metal to disappear. He wrote: "If you place a rod in the ground and electrically vibrated this rod, at first you would feel its oscillation. If it were vibrating a little faster you would expert to hear a hum coming from the shaft. Should it be heightened further, it would eventually become magnetic. By adding more resonance to the rod, it would begin to produce electrical energies. Further increasing the rod's intensity, would then cause its to become warm, proceeding onward through the temperature range, revealing colors associated with heat; red, orange, yellow, blue, violet, and so on.

"Then as the vibrations are augmented, it enters the radio spectrum, producing radio waves. Beyond that, it would enter the chemical range in the forty-eighth or forty-ninth octave. Still increasing the intensity of oscillation, it will begin to produce light around the fiftieth octave. A little higher up it goes into the realm of x-rays. Here, it would become dangerous to touch, or to be too near the rod.

"More rapid oscillations cause the rod to give off gamma rays which are very dangerous to the human form. Then proceeding on up higher in the spectrum, the so-called cosmic rays begin to make their presence known. So from a few vibrations a second, to countless millions (numbers with seventeen or eighteen decimals) the rod continues to blur as it vibrates with increasing intensity. Eventually, it will become invisible, and then who knows where it would go from there."

It's quite possible that UFOs, which appear suddenly in the sky, and just as suddenly disappear, operate on Bell's theory of extreme vibration. Of course, the occupants of the spacecraft must be capable of withstanding the enormous pressure, a feat which would kill humans.

INVISIBILITY AND LEVITATION

A startling photo taken by an unsuspecting visitor at high noon at the foot of Starr Hill in Warminster, U.K., depicts an object - a dark ominous shape - which the human eye was unable to detect. There on two different frames of 35mm film taken by John Wright was a giant black globe the likes of which were not observed. A check of the equipment showed no defect. When asked if he had noticed anything unusual at the time, Wright states he was aware only of the deathly silent and brooding atmosphere of his surroundings.

OUR "INVISIBLE" RESIDENTS

STARTLING NEW EVIDENCE... INVISIBLE UFO PHOTOGRAPHED ABOVE TINY ENGLISH TOWN AS FLYING SAUCER SIGHTINGS PERSIST

INVISIBILITY AND LEVITATION

EXOTIC TECHNOLOGY AND INVISIBILITY

In his book, *Flying Saucers on the Attack* (Citadel Press), Harold T. Wilkins writes that in both London and NY, attempts were made as far back as the 30's, to produce invisibility by warping light rays in an electromagnetic field. In 1934 in London, there was demonstrated in a public hall apparatus which was perhaps suggested by the fantasy of the late H.G. Wells' *"The Invisible Man."*

A young scientist, wearing what he called an Electro-Helmet and a special Mantle, went into a cabinet open at the front before a brilliantly lit stage. He then with both hands, touched contact gloves which were over his head.

An electric current was switched on and the man's body gradually vanished from feet to head. One could step up and touch him but could not see him. Nor did the camera reveal the secret, for it depicted only what the eye saw.

The inventor refused to reveal his secret which he said was the work of many years of experiments. All one could see was the development of a cone of light such as might be projected between the two poles of a powerful transmitter. This cone persisted even when the man could not be seen.

The inventor had succeeded in doing on stage in public what a dematerializing apparition is alleged to do in a haunted house. Whether he developed the powers of some new or previously discovered ray and created an opaque screen is hard to say. However, the inventor may have been the first to stumbled upon the science that years later would be developed for the infamous "Philadelphia Experiment."

INVISIBILITY AND LEVITATION

INVISIBLE FLYING OBJECTS

Catching a glimpse of a UFO is often a rare experience. If everyone could see UFOs darting about in our air space, there would be no doubts that UFOs exist. UFOs are classified as "phenomena" because sightings are rare (except in UFO hotspots) and there are so few witnesses. Many people have never seen a UFO and some people live their entire lives without ever seeing one. The rarity of observing UFOs, the lack of public acknowledgement that UFOs exist, government debunking and ridicule of witnesses who do come forward, and various human belief systems divide world populations into those who believe UFOs exist, those who do not and the "undecided."

Some researchers theorize that UFOs are multi-dimensional and appear and disappear when they "jump" from one dimension to another dimension. Other researchers believe UFO occupants use various frequencies of the electromagnetic spectrum to "cloak" their ships and thus create the illusion of invisibility.

UFOs may use a variety of EM frequencies to "cloak" their visibility and avoid detection. According to Ellen Crystall in her book *Silent Invasion* (Paragon House), "The ships release short wave radiation- ultraviolet, x-ray, and gamma ray - which our eyes do not see but which film registers." Crystall further states, "The ships' external covering has a quality that can render the ship invisible or transparent when lit. The ships' lights illuminate the portion of the ship immediately surrounding the lights. When a ship turns out all its lights, it seems to disappear as if dematerialized, but it has only vanished from our optical view not from our space-time."

In 1978, UFO researcher and publisher Timothy Green Beckley was investigating a series of amazing UFO sightings in the area surrounding Warminster, England. Beckley had gone to a remote hillside just outside of town where a number of UFO sightings had recently taken place. He was accompanied by Arthur Shuttlewood, Bob

INVISIBILITY AND LEVITATION

While UFO skywatching in Warminster, U.K. mysterious lights appeared on the right side of this photo taken by researcher Tim Beckley in the dead of night. Nothing was seen with the naked eye -- the film was not tampered with. Strange events of many types have transpired at this spot.

INVISIBILITY AND LEVITATION

Strong, and Eva Alcock.

During their hour-long watch on the hill Beckley took a photo of Bob Strong and Eva Alcock. Later, when the picture was developed, Beckley discovered a strange fleeting object behind the people in the photo. "There were no lights out there in the field. It was pitch black, yet there appears to be a bright form moving around in the background that comes down straight out of the sky." Apparently the camera had managed to catch something that was invisible to the human eye.

The use of EM frequencies to mask visibility may also be used by UFO occupants while outside the UFO. In a conscious encounter including multiple witnesses, photographs taken during the event display the image of a being with large, black eyes standing not more than 6-7 feet from the witness who took the photographs. However, according to the same witness, no such being was observed during the encounter. The photographer was actually attempting to photograph another being clearly visible and further away. The being in the photograph was not visible to the naked eye but was registered on film.

Another interesting case involving a strange image caught on film is the so-called "Cumbrian photograph." In 1964, Jim Templeton, a fire officer in the Cumbrain, England Fire Service, took a series of photographs while on a picnic with his family in the Burgh Marsh, a local Cumbrian beauty spot.

When the film was developed, the prints revealed something that was not seen at the time the picture was taken. The photo is of Templeton's five year old daughter, Elizabeth. What makes the picture so strange is that also seen in the background is a figure dressed in what appears to be a white "spacesuit" and wearing a helmet.

Jim Templeton said he was "flabbergasted." The only other people around were two ladies who sat in their car some three or four hundred yards away. Templeton recalled that the quiet was unusual. Normally there would be cows and sheep grazing everywhere. However on that particular day the only animals to be seen were huddled on the far side of the marsh.

The film company Kodak became involved with the photograph, even offering free film for life to anyone who could explain the picture, since they could find no evidence that the negative had been tampered with. Whatever it was that Jim Templeton accidentally caught on film that day, it evidently was invisible to the naked eye. Who or what on Earth has that kind of ability?

One theory often neglected in popular UFO literature concerns the reflective surface of UFOs often described by witnesses. Many observers describe UFOs as "mirror-like", "shiny", "reflective" and "like polished metal." The original sighting by Kennith Arnold in June of 1947 of nine UFOs over Mt. Ranier was typical of reports of highly reflective UFOs: "Every few seconds, two or three of them would dip or change their course slightly, just enough for the sun to catch their reflective surfaces."

Abductees also report observing UFOs with reflective surfaces during abduction experiences. In a childhood abduction, Betty Andreasson-Luca observed a round ship that was, "...silvery, sort of mirrorlike and transparent, and trees seemed to reflect in it." During his 1975 abduction experience, Travis Walton reported being taken to a larger ship where he observed various reflective objects in a hangar like room. Walton remembered, "On my left, toward one end of the large room, there were two or three oval-shaped saucers, reflecting light like highly polished chrome. I saw beyond the edge of the brushed-metal craft a silvery reflection that could have been another shiny, rounded craft."

UFOs may also use reflective properties to camouflage their presence and "blend

INVISIBILITY AND LEVITATION

While on a pleasant day's outing in the British country-side, Jim Templeton took this photo of his daughter near a nuclear power plant. When developed one of the photos taken showed a mysterious "invisible man" who had not been seen when the picture was taken.

in" with surroundings to avoid observation by human witnesses. Silvery, mirror-like surfaces would naturally reflect blue skies or other surroundings rendering the object virtually invisible. Unfortunately, the closer these objects come to light sources, such as the sun's corona, the less "camouflaged" these objects become and the easier they are to spot. UFO occupants may use all kinds of advanced technology to "cloak" their ships but we must not overlook the simple technique of camouflage used by even the tiniest of Nature's creatures.

UFOs may be rendered invisible through multidimensional travel, electromagnetic frequencies that "cloak" the objects, travel at speeds faster than the human eye can detect and even the use of reflective properties which serve to camouflage these objects. UFOs may not be invisible but rather unvisible to the human eye. As photographs and new techniques demonstrate, UFOs can become visible if we extend the visual range of the human eye through technology and other techniques. We may be looking right at the evidence but not seeing it. All we need now are the right tools to see beyond our physical, and sometimes mental limitations.

To induce Invisibility in matter, several techniques have been scientifically proven to accomplish that goal.

1. Bending light around the object so that it cannot contact
   the object and thus reflect back to the viewer

This principle takes advantage of the Refractive Index of a mass. All matter either reflects, diffuses or transmits light (indeed all radiation) to varying degrees based on its Refractive Index.

Refraction refers specifically to the change in direction of radiation, especially light, or sound frequencies as it passes obliquely from one medium to another resulting in a different propagation velocity. This change in the velocity (speed and direction) of the wave causes a corresponding change in the effective wavelength, thus the frequency of the radiation changes while moving within the medium. The degree of change is thus the Refractive Index.

The Refractive Index is the phase velocity of radiation if free space is divided by the phase velocity of the same radiation in a specified medium. The absolute index for all ordinary transparent substances is greater than 1, but there are some special cases (X-rays and light in metal films) for which the index of refraction is less than unity.

Now, if a means of "bending" all incoming visible wavelengths around an object were used, it would become invisible. The movie *Predator* takes this approach in the cloaking device which the alien wears. It could take the form of a fiber optic mesh or an electronic banding effect. If a high field density magnetic field is used, it would produce life altering effects on both the operator and the environment. Gravity waves might also be used to bend light around a person, thus creating invisibility.

Another method would be the use of a chemical, like that used in the movie "*The Invisible Man.*" Hopefully the effect would be non-toxic and wear off as the body eliminated the chemical over time.

As of now, there are no light-bending techniques which have worked. It is always possible that some researcher or group of researchers has achieved this and is keeping it quiet.

2. Shifting to a higher form of energy which cannot be seen.

INVISIBILITY AND LEVITATION

There is mention of a technique related to possible invisibility fields produced by UFOs. It involves the stimulation of a mass to a frequency in either the Infrared, Ultraviolet or higher frequencies.

There are several interesting points when looking at it from this angle. ultraviolet (UV) light sucks heat from the body while infrared (IR) light projects heat into the body. If all visible light reflected from an object could be stepped up to a doubling or a harmonic outside the bounds of the visible spectrum (this could be either Ultra or Infra), then the object would appear as a black hole in the shape of the object.

If IR was used, then the object would give off heat. If UV was used, people in the presence of the operator would experience burns and conjunctivitis (burning, reddening and swelling of the eyes). Many UFO close encounters have as a physical side effect, the burning of the skin and eye swelling. This indicates a high proportion of UV or other higher radiation.

To cause the body to emit frequencies beyond the visible spectrum, one could use a super-heterodyne effect or some form of doubling or tripling. Crystals could be used for achieving the doubling. While super- heterodyning would be accomplished by the blending of two or more frequencies to generate both the sum and difference frequencies.

I don't see how this technique could work if the sole result is to delineate a black human shape. The invisibility would be defeated since the object would be so obvious, if not totally conspicuous.

There is the possibility that there are principles of light which we don't completely understand. This could be especially true at Ultraviolet, Infrared, and other unseen frequencies. For that reason, this possible technique should be looked into.

INVISIBILITY AND LEVITATION

3. Dimensional shifting of the object itself

If the object could be so "excited" as to translate to a higher dimension or level of being, then it would effectively not be respondent to radiations, including light, from this dimension. One case involved certain experiments using high density fluctuating magnetic fields.

A device was built in the shape of a split-phase coil with many turns of wire. When the subject sat astraddle the coil and the power was applied, at certain frequencies and magnetic field densities, the subject saw the room slowly vanish to be displaced by other scenery.

Further experiments caused the subject and the coil to begin to vanish from the test area. The subject obviously "translated" to a higher dimension, both visually and physically. This might not be the rule for all such experiments. There is much work to be done using different frequencies, combinations of such and field densities.

It might be possible to cause a "vanishing" without losing the physical form. One of the communications given to UFO contact Billy Meier stated that the Pleidians used a time shifting technique. This allowed them to vanish and reappear in another location almost instantly.

They said time could be divided into many separate and distinct moments, each of which could house an entire universe co-existent with ours, yet totally unknown and unsuspected by us. Perhaps this theory explains how UFO's, Bigfoot, Loch Ness and other anomalies occur in our reality. They are momentarily "displaced" entities from another dimension.

INVISIBILITY AND LEVITATION

It would follow that phase conjugate techniques could be used to energize an area to a level of very high field density. If something walked into that field as it "scanned" another dimension, it could be "charged" to forcibly drag it into our dimension. When this occurs, the being is disturbed and confused by this seemingly "magical" accident.

As time progressed, the energy charge would fade away and the entity would reach the quantum level necessary to cause the return to their home dimension. This of course could work the other way. Perhaps some of the thousands of people who turn up missing each year have been carried into some other dimension, never to be seen again.

Writer, Arthur Shuttlewood experienced numerous UFO-related phenomenon while investigating the UFO flap over Warminster, England in 1972. Some of his unusual sightings involved UFOs and weird creatures that seemed to utilize invisibility of some kind. "Events of the last few months have helped to steadily convince me that a sizeable portion of what has transpired in and around Warminster, is of a non-physical nature, totally defying the laws of science. We now have strong evidence that some of these aeroforms are capable of making themselves invisible."

Shuttlewood maintained that under certain circumstances these "invisible" UFOs and their crew members can be seen with the aid of photographic equipment or by individuals who happen to visually catch them while they are in the process of making a transformation from visibility to invisibility.

During the winter of 1972, Shuttlewood was able to see for himself the strange nature of the mysterious visitors. "It was about 8:30PM. I was on Starr Hill along with a half-dozen other individuals, including a former police officer and a bank executive. Suddenly, we heard thumping noises from a clump of bushes to our left. Another sound caused us all to look at the hedgerow to our left. That's when we saw the three giant figures standing at the edge of a field some distance away. They were all eight feet tall, had domed heads, no apparent necks, wide shoulders, and long arms that dangled at their sides. Their outlines were clearly discernible even though it was dark, the strange thing was that you could see right through them."

As the startled observers attempted to leave the area the transparent "creatures" followed them, gliding several inches above the ground. "We attempted to communicate with them, but they did not respond. A member of our party walked right up to one of these beings and was able to pass right through the eerie form. The figures vanished as the lights of approaching cars moved in our direction."

Sightings of transparent creatures around the nearby Cradle Hill were also reported. Sally Pike, daughter of retired Police Superintendent John Rossiter, gave the following details of her strange experiences. "Both my husband and I have had rather unnerving experiences at Cradle Hill. One evening, I saw quite clearly the outline of a tall male figure striding up the road in the bright moonlight. He seemed about seven feet tall, with extremely long arms. His body itself, only the outline being solid, was almost transparent and silverish. As I watched, he slowly faded away and vanished."

Mrs. Pike's husband, Neal, would encounter a similar being several days later. "As I approached the white metal gates which lead to Cradle Hill, I suddenly saw three giant figures standing in a line. At first they were mere shadowy, ghostlike outlines. But, as I peered through the darkness, they sharpened their form until they appeared almost solid. The unusual thing was that their bodies ended at the mid-section, no legs or feet were visible."

Wondering if his eyes were playing tricks on him, Neal aimed his flashlight at one of the creatures. Immediately the giant vanished, only to reappear at another spot. "I flashed my searchlight onto the two other forms, and the same thing happened. The ghostly trio were now much closer to me, their faces featureless, black and fearsome." Neal Pike decided that he had seen enough, and quickly fled Cradle Hill.

INVISIBILITY AND LEVITATION

It was at this UFO "hot spot" just outside of Warminster,
England that witnesses -- including local banking officials
-- swear that transparent beings from a landed UFO
actually walked right through this fence becoming
totally invisible at one point.

INVISIBILITY AND LEVITATION

Research done by Shuttlewood showed that a total of seventeen people had seen the gigantic, transparent beings on Cradle and Starr Hills. "There was something strange going on in Warminster. It may be that an armada of spaceships and their crews were using our town as a landing base or way station. There is now substantial evidence to indicate that they are able to make themselves invisible upon command. We can only guess as to what their purpose might be. Let us hope it is a peaceful one."

UFOnauts have obviously mastered the art of invisibility as well as levitation. Eyewitnesses have seen visitors from outer space levitating outside their spaceships. Earthlings have experienced being levitated from the ground and into the opening of ships for visits. UFOs on the ground have been seen to rise up without the use of any power, rocket or otherwise. How is it done? Is levitation too far-fetched an answer? We think not.

EDI - - - AN OTHER-WORLDLY ENIGMA

Edi lives in South America. She is about 30 years old with a pretty face and rich black hair that tumbles to her waist. Edi is an accountant for a major industry in Bolivia. Ever since she has been old enough to think for herself she has felt that she was put on Earth to carry out a special mission. What that assignment is, is not entirely clear to her as yet. She does have two clues. One is that she is adept at math. The other is a peculiar birthmark on her back. An astronomer has studied the mark and believes that it matches a major constellation in space.

Noted investigator Bill Cox who wrote about Edi in his book, *Unseen Kingdoms* (Inner Light Publications) thinks Edi may actually be a "walk-in," an entity from another world, and that her birthmark is a sign to others that they have found a comrade. Apparently, she is "marked" for a definite reason. Edi has already been contacted by other "walk-ins" who have greeted her without really telling her what her mission is. Edi has some theories of her own, but she refuses to speculate publicly.

For example, a few years ago Edi was stopped on the street by a man in his fifties. He had white hair and a white beard. He had approached her from behind and therefore "saw" the mark on her back. Incredibly, he called her by name, saying: Edi, you are one of us. . . you have the birthmark on your back."

Edi had never seen the man before, but the amazing part of the story was that he could not have seen the birthmark because Edi was wearing a dress with covered it. The man told her, "I'm to give you this book. Keep it as long as you want. It contains the information you need because your work begins as of now."

He told Edi that he was from the same constellation as her, and then showed a birthmark on his arm that matched hers perfectly.

Edi read the book, then reread it. The information in it was interesting but not world-shaking. In fact, she kept it in her home for a year and a half before picking it up again.

The message for her was on the first page. She now knew what she had to do. Weeks later she brought the book to work, and on her way home she heard a voice say, "Thank you for returning the book." She turned around and saw a white-bearded man. What perplexed Edi was how the man knew she had the book in her purse.

She gave him the book. He then told her, "You will be contacted again soon." Several months later Edi was in La Paz, Bolivia on an assignment for her employer. She was in a hotel restaurant eating dinner alone and not thinking about much of anything. Suddenly, a man approached her. He was extremely tall, about six feet seven inches, and good looking. He too, knew her name. He said, "Edi, I am glad to see you here, may I sit down?" He smiled at her and continued, "I know about your birthmark. I have one too."

Edi was not thrilled, she intended to say no to the stranger, but he did appear sincere. The blond man said, "I don't want you to think that I wish to invade your mind, but I read your thoughts, and it's OK. Am I correct?" Then he sat down and rolled up his sleeve. The birthmark was on the inside of his left forearm, and it was exactly the same as the one on Edi's back.

The next day the blond man took Edi to an ancient site in Bolivia called Tihuanacu. Archaeologists are puzzled by the ruins. However, UFOlogists believe it is an ancient Initiatic and Sacred Ceremonial city. The feeling is that Tihuanacu was a favorite landing area for ancient astronauts.

By now however, Edi was curious about her new friend. If he were really sent to Earth by a superior power, then he would have to prove it. At her request, the man smiled and promptly levitated his body into the air. Next he levitated a large, heavy stone.

The man said, "Edi, you must now learn the power of your mind. I want you to mentally raise the stone."

The women said, "But I can't levitate things."

"Yes, you can." He raised the stone again, and after a few minutes Edi was able to the same, although it did wobble and sink back to the ground. What she did was to keep the stone levitated after the blond man raised it up, but she was successful in only holding it in the air with his help. He told her that she would learn to do it by herself eventually. Then he took her on a tour of the ruins, explaining how their forefathers landed in that area eon's ago, and used levitation to lift the heavy rocks to build the impressive structures.

Also in *Unseen Kingdoms*, Bill Cox tells about Paul, a South American "spaceman" who is setting up a research center in Brasilia, Brazil.

THE UNCANNY PAUL LAUSSAC - - - SPACEMAN

According to Bill, Paul Laussac is financially secure. What he wants to do is serve humanity. Money is not his goal. Paul has a giving nature. Like most New Age people, he does not chase the dollar, but instead, chases after anything that will improve mankind. For that reason he created the research center.

Paul has the uncanny ability to appear, or not to appear, in any photo taken of him. If he chooses, he will be seen only as energy on film. Bill Cox, who spent a lot of time in South America, says that a few of the spacemen he met in Brazil have the same ability.

Cox says: "I've been in photos with Paul where my own body began to disappear because specialized energy extended from his body into my own auric field. It is hard to get a good picture of him in focus because he is so often in a different state of vibration than we might expect in ordinary human terms.

"Although our naked eye doesn't see these energies, " says Cox, "just as the tape recorder in voice tape phenomena records voices and sounds from other dimensions we

INVISIBILITY AND LEVITATION

don't ordinarily hear. In other words, these energies function in the sub-audible or super-audible ranges, giving us extended hearing, and wider vision in the ultra-violet and infra-red spectra. We see only within a very small range of a vastly greater visual scale. There are other octaves of vision. Clairvoyants, clairaudients and certain instruments record frequencies of seeing and hearing that have little to do with infra-red or ultra-violet. They are obviously registering sights and sounds perceived in the higher octaves of light and color, music and sound. People with ultra-sensitive hearing may be clairaudient, that is, hearing broadcasts without radio; voices and music from the spheres."

ACHIEVING INVISIBILITY INSIDE A PYRAMID

Bill Cox published a newsletter called *The Pyramid Guide*. He's had letters from all over the world, and has had people visit him to learn more about the magic of the pyramid.

About six years ago some California architects asked him to meet with them at Pepperdine University in Malibu. They had built an interlaced, rod framework of tetrahedrons which made up a pyramid about 30 feet high. It was covered with nylon. Bill Cox told me that he frequently gets a photographic phenomenon under a pyramid in which it appears that the individuals being photographed are becoming invisible.

He calls this "solarization." He says that the subjects inside and outside the pyramid are in different states of vibration. The body energy of those inside alters the photographic result. For some reason, a solarization effect takes place on the film, but the boundaries of that effect are restricted to bodies only. If this had been due to defects on the film, or processing errors, the entire photo frame would exhibit solarization throughout. This is not the case. One photo clearly shows three individuals actually fading from view, although the rest of the picture is perfectly clear.

INVISIBILITY AND LEVITATION

There are those who insist that the blocks that
go to make up the pyramids
of Egypt must have been levitated into place.

INVISIBILITY AND LEVITATION

Ancient Egyptian legends state that those who knew the secret, could become invisible by entering the pyramids via secret passageways known only to the high-priests. Upon entry, certain rituals must be performed to allow the pyramid energy to flow through the body. Invisibility was accomplished until the sun rose in the morning.

THE EXTRAORDINARY POWERS OF TOMAS GREEN CONTINHO

Bill Cox's book **Unseen Kingdoms** gives us a glimpse of a man who is a super levitator, super alchemist and super spaceman. His name is Tomas Green Coutinho and his home is in Tres Corazones, Brazil. He is able to levitate chairs even if they are nailed to the floor. Cox saw him pick up a fork between his thumb and forefinger - - - then watched it double over, break, and fall to the floor in droplets of metal, as though it had been subjected to intense heat.

Transmutation (alchemy) is no problem for Tomas. He can change buttons into coins. Not only that, he can change the button into any kind of coin you ask for. Tomas has transmuted a $20 (Brazilian cruzeiros) bill into butter, and then change d it back again.

Tomas Coutinho has followers, but most of them are UFOs. A photograph of this amazing man will invariably show UFOs in the background of the picture. What's more, the ships are in focus and quite clear. One might see a mother ship with smaller craft coming out of her belly.

Bill Cox wrote an extensive article about Tomas for the **UFO Review** titled "*Spaceman Show Us Your Powers*." In it, Cox wrote: "Claims made by others for Tomas' extraordinary powers include the following: That he welds metals together or separates fused metals with mind power alone; charges all types of batteries applying the same phenomenal powers; transforms cotton into metal, and vice-versa; turns ashes into money, even enlarging or diminishing the object in size as he performs the mental act, and then turns the transmuted artifact back into its original state again, never touching the object, and achieving this feat while the specimen is even held in the hands of the astounded subject; and other unbelievable demonstrations."

Bill Cox tells an amusing story about a man who attended group meetings held by Tomas. Tomas performed his phenomenal acts for the group, but the man said he could no longer come to the meetings because his wife was not convinced of Tomas' powers. Tomas invited her to see for herself. She refused, saying: "If Tomas can truly bend metal with his mind, let him come here to our house, where I can control the conditions and stop the fakery."

The young man explained to Tomas that he was in a dilemma. Would he come to his house? If Tomas did not come, then it was likely that the young man would not be able to attend any of the meetings.

Tomas was silent for awhile, then thrust his right hand forward and cried, "Hah!" He said to the young man, "It's OK now. Don't worry, she won't be a problem."

The man didn't know what he was talking about until he went home. His wife met him at the door holding a twisted fork. In stony silence she motioned for him to follow her, which he did. Then he saw that in all of the open drawers there were bent and twisted silverware and household utensils. The wife from then on was a true believer and even attended meetings.

Bill Cox said that Tomas could sharpen dull cutlery with intense mind focus. The pharmacist, in his mid-thirties, could also drive a car blindfolded on a winding mountain road. He was able to engage or disengage the moving parts of a car at will, without touching them. Once, Tomas made a quick, right-hand maneuver with the steering wheel while in traffic, yet the car continued on straight forward as though the wheel had been tightly held. At another time, while under strict laboratory conditions, Tomas placed an unoccupied car through several highway maneuvers, starting, stopping, turning and braking the car solely with the power of his mind.

: The Ascension (1:9–11).

STRANGE, EERIE, AND PECULIAR TALENTS

INVISIBILITY AND LEVITATION

Levitation can be defined as the paranormal suspension of the human body in midair. For example, "simple" levitations are instances in which a Saint or holy man will become buoyant and will suddenly float up into the air, usually against his will.

Accounts also describe the "spiritual flights" of levitating mystics and yogis who, after becoming airborne, have found themselves flying through the sky. There are also cases on record of deliberately induced levitation, a phenomenon often produced by yogis.

Newton's law of gravity does not always work. There are some humans who defy the law without meaning to. They apparently have no control over themselves and will float skyward without expending any effort. Madame Alexandra David-Neal, the French explorer who spent 14 years in Tibet, relates a strange case in her book, *Mystere et magique en Tibet*.

She wrote that she had once seen a naked man weighed down with heavy chains. A friend of his told the author that because of intense mystical training, his body had become so light that if he didn't drape himself in chains he would float away.

Stories about human levitation are not rare. It is perhaps the most commonly mentioned miracle in yogic and Tibetan Buddhist Literature and in the lore of the Roman Catholic Saints. In his book, *The Wonders of the Saints*, the Reverend F. Fielding-Ould notes that:

"When we turn to the records of the Church, we find the same phenomenon observed in many instances. St. Ignatius Loyola, the founder of the Society of Jesus, was, while at prayer, seen by one John Pascal to be raised more than a foot above the ground. St. Phillip Neri was levitated 'about a palm' from his sickbed, in full view of his attendants. St. Joseph of Copertino while celebrating the Mysteries in 1649 before

INVISIBILITY AND LEVITATION

The reported instances of levitation can be found in many ancient texts as well as modern literature on the paranormal

INVISIBILITY AND LEVITATION

the Duke of Brunswick, was bodily raised a hand's breadth above the level of the alter, and remained there six or seven minutes. St. James of Illyricum was levitated while at prayer; St. Dominic at the Holy Communion, a cubit from the ground. Much the same thing is told of St. Dunstan, St. Phillip Benite, St. Cajetan, St. Albert of Sicily, and St. Bernard Ptolomaei. St. Richard, his chancellor testifies that he saw St. Edmund, Archbishop of Canterbury, "raised high in the air with knees bent and arms stretched out."

St. Joseph of Copertino, who lived from 1603 to 1663, reportedly had little control over his levitations. Every time he became excited he would drift off the ground. Some say that this simple peasant from Apulia, Italy, was feeble-minded. Nevertheless, even as a youngster he tried desperately to reach religious ecstasy by whipping himself, starvation, and by wearing hair shirts. At the age of 22 he became a Franciscan monk.

It was then that the levitations grew more and more frequent. During Mass on a Sunday he rose out of his pew and flew to the alter where many candles were burning. Some of them burned Joseph quite seriously. After that episode he was no longer permitted to take part in public services.

However, the levitations continued. One day while walking with a Benedictine monk he became excited and flew up into a tree. Unfortunately, he could not fly back down again; someone had to get a ladder and assist him back down to the ground.

The many witnesses to St. Joseph's levitations were two cardinals, a surgeon, and Pope Urban VIII. He spent his entire life in prayer and was canonized because the Church felt that his levitations had to be the work of God.

INVISIBILITY AND LEVITATION

* * *

MEDALLION HONORING FLYING SAINTS

INVISIBILITY AND LEVITATION

THE REAL FLYING NUN

Her name was St. Teresa of Avila. She died in 1582. She was another holy person who levitated involuntarily. She wrote: "It seemed to me, when I tried to make some resistance, as if a great force beneath my feet lifted me up. . . I confess that it threw me into great fear, very great indeed at first; for in seeing one's body thus lifted up from the earth, though the spirit draws it upwards after itself (and that with great sweetness, if unresisted) the senses are not lost; at least I was so much myself as able to see that I was being lifted up. After the rapture was over, I have to say my body seemed frequently to be buoyant, as if all weight had departed form it, so much so that now and then I scarce knew my feet touched the ground."

St. Teresa often felt an "attack" coming on. At such times she would ask the sisters to hold her down. However, there were too many occasions when no one was nearby, and so the woman soared through the air.

St. Teresa, the famous reformer of the Carmelite order, talked also of rapture. "During rapture, the soul does not seem to animate the body. . .A rapture is absolutely irresistible, whilst union, inasmuch as we are still as on our own ground, may be hindered, though that resistance be painful and violent; it is, however, almost always impossible. But rapture, for the most part, is irresistible. It comes, in general, as a shock, quick and sharp, before you can collect your thoughts or help yourself in any way, and you see and feel it as a cloud or a strong eagle rising upwards and carrying you away on its wings."

The Saint's most famous levitation occurred during a conversation with St. John of the Cross, who had come to the convent of the Incarnation to visit her. While John spoke of the Trinity, St. Teresa knelt in prayer. Suddenly, John was rapt in ecstasy. He rose from the floor, taking his chair with him. St. Teresa was also lifted into the air. This is one of the few cases of double levitations ever recorded.

INVISIBILITY AND LEVITATION

Sister Anne was another eyewitness to one of St. Teresa's levitations. She made her deposition thirty years after St. Teresa's death. The occasion was an inquiry at Segovia. Sister Anne, under oath, stated:

"On another occasion, between one and two o'clock in the daytime, I was in the choir waiting for the bell to ring, when our Holy Mother entered and knelt down for perhaps the half of a quarter of an hour. As I was looking on, she was raised about half a yard from the ground without her feet touching it. At this I was terrified, and she, for her part, was trembling all over. So I moved to where she was, and I put my hands under her feet, over which I remained weeping for something like a half an hour while the ecstasy lasted. Then suddenly she sank down and rested on her feet, and turning to me, she asked who I was, and ordered me under obedience to say nothing of what I had seen, and I have, in fact, said nothing until the present moment."

Rabi'a al-Adawiyya al-Qaysiyya was born and lived in the town of Basra, in present-day Iraq. We know little of her actual life. She apparently was born into a poor family, orphaned at a young age, separated from her sisters, and sold into slavery. Her master, perceiving her special qualities, set her free - whereupon she devoted herself, with uncompromising dedication, to the highest spiritual development. She was offered money, houses, marriage proposals. Yet she chose to remain single and live a simple, humble life. She became famous during her life as a saint, and quickly became regarded as one of the major saints of Islam and foremost figures of the Sufi tradition.

The little that we know of Rabi'a takes the form of stories of her interactions with other people - stories that have been passed down through generations of Sufi writers. A small body of poetical prose is also attributed to her. One of the best-known stories about Rabi'a centers around an interaction with Hasan of Basra, a well-known religious leader of the time. A humorous story, it tells how Hasan tried to exploit Rabi'a's special powers for his own glory:

INVISIBILITY AND LEVITATION

One day Hasan saw Rabi'a among a group of people near the riverside. Approaching her, Hasan threw his prayer rug on the surface of the water and said, "Rabi'a, come and let us pray together here." He did this in order to display his mastery over the element of water. "Hasan," Rabi'a replied, "When you display your spiritual goods in this worldly market, you should display things that your fellow men are incapable of displaying." Then she threw her prayer rug into the air and flew up to it. "Come up here, Hasan, where people can see us!" she called. Unable to do so, Hasan said nothing. "Hasan," Rabi'a said, wishing to comfort him, "do you need to use a spiritual gift to gain a worldly reputation? What you can do, fish can also do, and what I can do, flies can also do. The real work lies beyond both of these. We should devote ourselves to the real work."

THE STRANGE POSSESSION OF FRANCOIS FONTAINE

Records show that not all levitations are performed by Saints and other holy men, but can also be demonic in origin. Sulpitius Severus described his observations of St. Martin when he approached a person possessed by unholy beings. Severus said, "The demoniac raised from the earth and remained suspended in the air, with his arms stretched out, without touching the ground with his feet . . . You could see the wretched person whirled about in different ways, uplifted and floated in the air with feet upwards"

An even stranger case occurred in Louviers, France, in 1591. The incident was recorded in an official report which is in the Bibliotheque Nationale of Paris. It concerns the possession of a girl named Francois Fontaine. The report reads:

"And having entered the court, the door of which is under the porch and in the passage of the prison, Francois walked but six paces into the court, and we together with our clerk entered the office where the judge's chair is and the sitting is held, and, as our clerk was beginning to writhe the present report that we were dictating to him, he cried out and showed us Francois, who was near the door of the court, whom we all saw raised about two feet off the floor, upright, and at once she fell down on the ground, flat on the back, with her arms spread out crosswise, and afterwards she was dragged, with her head foremost, still on her back, along the court, without anybody touching her or standing near her, as witnessed La Prime, the jailer, Nicolas Pellet, servant of the jailer, his wife and several prisoners who came into the court, a thing which amazed us much."

In an attempt to exorcise the demon in the girl, the Provost read the Gospel of St. John. The girl was on the floor stretched out on her back. Suddenly, she raised up, horizontally, for about three or four feet, and was carried by some unseen force toward the exorcist, who fled to his office in terror.

The report states: ". . .as we continued to read the Gospel of St. John, the body of Francois, who was then lying on the ground, face upwards, began to crawl along, head foremost, all disheveled and bristly, and all at once the body of Francois was raised off the floor, three or four feet high, and borne horizontally, face upwards along the court, without anything to support her. When we saw the body make straight for us, thus suspended in midair, it threw us into such a fright that we withdrew into the office of the court, locking the door behind us and reading the Gospel of St. John down to the end.

"But the body kept following us through the air up to the office, against the door of which it struck with the soles of its feet, and then was carried back through the air, with the face upwards and head foremost, out of the court. This gave such a fright to the jailer, her servants, our archers and many prisoners who were present with several inhabitants of Louviers, that they fled, some into the prison, some into the street, after shutting the doors behind them; and the body of Francois was carried away out of the court and remained in the passage of the prison, between the door of it and the street door which the fugitives had shut in their flight. We considered this with great astonishment, till one Desjardins and other prisoners opened the door of the prison and said they would help us, which enabled us to get out of the office and court, having thus found Francois lying on the ground close to the prison door."

Later on an attempt was made to give her the Holy Sacrament as a means of chasing the demon away. It didn't work. The demon's power was mightier than the exorcist. The report says: "And Francois, kneeling down, had been most alarmingly carried away, without being able to take the Sacrament, opening her mouth, rolling her eyes in her head in such a horrible way that it had been necessary, with the help of five of six persons, to pull her down by her dress as she was raised into the air, and they had thrown her down on the floor . . .Then the cure had presented the Holy Host again to Francois, who had knelt down; but she was again snatched off the floor, higher than the alter, as if she had been taken by the hair, in such a strange way that the bystanders were much amazed, and would never have thought of witnessing so frightful a thing, and they all knelt and began saying prayers. . ."

The cure Pellet made still another attempt to give the girl Holy Communion, and "she had been for the third time prevented from taking it, having been for the third time carried over a large bench that was before the alter where Mass was said, and lifted up into the air towards where a glass had been broken, with her head downwards and her feet upwards, without her clothes being upset, through which, before and behind, was belching forth much water and stinking smoke. . .and for some time thus carried through the air, till at last seven or eight men had taken hold of her and brought her down to the ground."

The report does not tell us what eventually happened to Francois Fontaine. We can only hope that the demon left her body and that she returned to a normal life. What the story does tell, however, is that the power of levitation is not exclusive to Saints and other holy people. The power could be dormant in all of us, needing only the proper catalyst to set it into action.

THE
ENIGMA OF
DANIEL DOUGLAS HOME

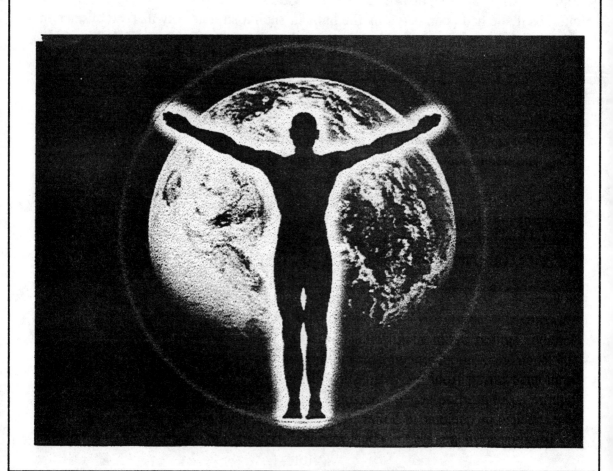

INVISIBILITY AND LEVITATION

D.D. Home was a Spiritualist born in Scotland in 1833 and was brought up in America. As a child he was sickly and possibly suffered from attacks of hysteria. The first hint of his psychic ability came when he was 13. He had a vision of his friend, Edwin. He told his family that Edwin had been dead for three days. Home was right. News came that Edwin had died three days earlier.

Home's psychic powers developed through his teen years. Before he died at the age of 53, he was noted for being able to perform three types of miracles: He was able to handle fire without burning himself, levitate at will, and to move heavy objects without touching them physically.

Home was 34 in 1867 when he met young Lord Adare, a British correspondent for the *Daily Telegraph*. There were several other witnesses in the room when Home stirred the embers in the fireplace with his hands, keeping both hands in the flames until the embers caught. He then placed his face in the glowing embers, moving it about as though bathing it in water. His flesh was examined by witnesses, but no one could find any evidence of charring.

Later that night Home held a glowing ember in his hands for several minutes. It was so hot that no one else could come within four or five inches of it without pulling back.

Home rubbed elbows with the great figures of the day, Napoleon III, the Empress Eugenie, Count Alexis Tolstoy, Elizabeth Barrett Browning and William Makepeace Thackeray. Thomas Trollope, brother of the novelist Anthony, decided to check up on Home by talking to the most famous stage magician of the period, Bartolomeo Bosco. Bosco said that there was absolutely no trickery that he could see in Home's performance. No mere conjurer could match Home's miracles. The amazing miracles were never performed on a stage. Home preferred someone's parlor, and he liked to have influential people as witnesses. Nor did he ever accept money for his work.

INVISIBILITY AND LEVITATION

HOME'S FEATS OF LEVITATION

On scores of occasions Home rose straight up into the air and floated about the room to the amazement of guests. Often, these witnesses would pass their hands around his while he was suspended in mid-air. He once rose so high that he made a chalk mark on the ceiling.

One guest on this occasion was a skeptical reporter named F.L. Burr, editor of the *Hartford Times*. He wrote later:

"Suddenly, without any expectation on the part of the company, Home was taken up into the air. I had hold of his hand at the time and I felt his feet. . .they were lifted a foot from the floor. He palpitated from head to foot with the contending emotions of joy and fear which choked his utterances. Again and again he was taken from the floor, and the third time he was carried to the ceiling of the apartment, with which his hands and feet came into gentle contact."

Home's most famous feat of levitation occurred on December 16, 1868. Three reputable witnesses were present, Lord Adare, the Master of Lindsay, and Captain Wynne. All of them watched in astonishment as D. D Home floated into the air, went out one window and floated back into another. The windows of the fashionable London home were 80 feet high.

Home had conducted more than 1,500 seances and had never been detected as a fraud. However, this business of floating out of one window and back into another was hard for most people to believe. Suspicion arouse when it was learned that Home insisted that his three witnesses remain seated until he re-emerged through the window. Being English gentlemen, they obeyed. What would they have seen, however, had they rushed to the window and looked out? Would they have seen Home walking a

INVISIBILITY AND LEVITATION

Medium Daniel Douglas Home levitated to the
ceiling numerous times, placing chalk
marks to show his feats of levitation
were not being hoaxed.

tightrope? Or swinging by a rope to the other window? The answer will never be known.

The three witnesses were convinced that true levitation had occurred. Lord Adare wrote in a book devoted to Home: "Presently Home appeared, standing upright, outside our window. He opened the window and came in quite coolly. I went with him into the next room. The window was not raised a foot. . .He then went out through the space, head first, his body being horizontal and apparently rigid. He came in again, feet foremost."

The Master of Lindsay said: "We heard the window in the next room lifted up, and almost immediately after saw Home floating in the air outside our window. He remained in this position a few seconds, then raised the window and glided into the room, feet foremost, and sat down."

In a letter to Home, the third witness, Captain Charles Wynne, said: "I don't think anyone who knows me would for a moment say I was a victim to hallucination or any other humbug of the kind. The fact of your having gone out of the window and in the other, I can swear to."

D.D. Home once accomplished a Houdini-like feat that would have made the great escape artist envious. The incident was reported by Mr. Sergeant Cox, a respected member of the bar. Cox was in the room with chemist Sir William Crookes; his brother, Walter, and famed ethnologist and traveler E. Galton.

These four men were the testers. They tied Home to a chair with tightly wound copper wire. The psychic's wrist and ankles were bound. The chair was then wired to an iron gate and all the joints were soldered. A dressing gown was placed on top and the sleeves were sewn together. The windows and doors to the room were locked.

INVISIBILITY AND LEVITATION

Home could not move any part of his body.

The testers moved to the next room, which was separated by an archway and a curtain. This room was fully lighted with gas burners. Four minutes of silence followed. Then a bell in Home's room was rung. A chair, a footstool and other pieces of furniture were pushed through the curtain.

Sergeant Cox wrote: "Presently, the curtains were partially drawn, and there was a man, dressed like a sailor, but whose features were exactly like those of Home. We were all satisfied it was indeed Home. He stood there talking to us for half an hour, answering questions. I said, 'Are you substantial or only a shape?' 'I am as solid as you are,' was the answer. Then he said, 'Will you thrust your finger in my mouth?' He opened his jaws and I thrust in my finger. He gave me a bite that made me cry. Having held me thus for nearly a minute, he let go, and with a loud laugh said, ' Do you call that psychic force?'"

The four men then went through the curtain. Cox wrote: "The psychic (Home) was as we left him, only in a state of unconsciousness. The wires were uncut, the solder perfect, the chair bound to the gate, the dressing gown upon him. The door was locked, the seals upon it and the window unbroken. He was wearing the dress suit in which we had tied him up."

Apparently, Daniel Dunglas Home was able to communicate with the dead. When his fame spread throughout London he was invited into homes at the rate of six or seven times a week, conducting seances to amuse and startle his followers. For that service he was fed, clothed and kept in pocket money. The wealthy and influential adored him.

107

INVISIBILITY AND LEVITATION

DISCIPLE OF EVIL?

Eventually, Homes set his sights on Europe, and gained more conquests. In 1855 he went to Florence, Italy, and was the guest of the mother of novelist Anthony Trolope. From there he went to Naples and stayed with a noble Polish family. In Rome, he wanted desperately to become a Catholic. However, here he ran into a snag. The Church knew all about D.D. Home. It did not think he made a good subject for conversion. The chief of the inquisition made him sign a document which read:

"I Daniel Dunglas Home, hereby solemnly declare and avow that I have not sold my soul to the Devil, nor have I on any occasion been cognizant of holding communications with the Evil One. - - - Rome, March 18, 1856."

The following year the urge to embrace Catholicism may have faded. He was now holding seances for the Emperor Napoleon III and his Empress Eugenie. He permitted them to touch spirit hands. Home also materialized the hand of Napoleon Bonaparte, which grabbed a pencil and scrawled his signature. Later it was verified as being his.

Palace gates were opened to him. Home walked the huge rooms of mansions belonging to great financiers. Witnesses claimed his mediumship was something to behold. When Home went into a trance, musical instruments played, floating in the air. Bells rang. Solid objects appeared from nowhere. Tables rose off the floor. D.D. Home was able to stretch his body from three to five inches, to the astonishment of doctors and scientists. He could also shrink himself by as many inches.

On another trip to Rome, he fell in love with a wealthy Russian girl. Twelve days later they were engaged, but the Czar had to give his approval. For Home, that was no problem. He went to Peterhof Palace and dazzled the Czar with his occult powers. Consent was given, along with a large diamond ring. Another ring was given by the

INVISIBILITY AND LEVITATION

Czar when the couple's baby was born.

Unfortunately things started going wrong for Home. In 1864 the Church of Rome branded him as a disciple of the devil. He was, the Church stated, a sorcerer. Home had to leave Rome in a hurry. Then his wife died. Her family tightened the reins on the family fortune and it was necessary for the psychic to sue. The suit was settled in his favor. However, that was followed by another suit, this one from the woman who had adopted him as her son. Over the years she had given him gifts valued at sixty thousand pounds. Now she wanted them back, and she won her case in court.

Undaunted, Home went to Russia, where he found a wealthy woman willing to marry him. He spent years in Russia, amusing his hosts and hostesses in wealthy and fashionable homes.

Back in England in 1870, Home was in trouble. There was a popular clamor for an investigation of this man who could levitate and speak to the dead. The one chosen to do the job was Sir William Crookes, a brilliant chemist and physicist. Crookes was the inventor of the x-ray tube which still bears his name today.

To do the job properly, Crookes used a great deal of apparatus, much of it designed especially for the experiments. He wrote about his results in the July 1, 1871 issue of the *Quarterly Journal of Science*. In his article, Crookes stated that under conditions of perfect control, Home had floated in the air supported by an unknown force. He had handled red hot coals without injury, and objects near Home had moved by themselves.

Tragically, that report dogged Crookes to his grave. He was stigmatized as having been a fool and a dupe. Still, he refused to change his mind. Twenty years later he wrote: "I find nothing to retract or to alter. I have discovered no flaw in the experiments then made, or in the reasoning I based on them."

INVISIBILITY AND LEVITATION

D.D. Home died at Auteuil near Paris in 1886. For some thirty years he had lived a life of ease, doing nothing more strenuous than holding seances. The tragedy is that he might have taken his mediumship to great heights if he had chosen to do something other than entertain the wealthy.

Table tipping has often been thought of as a cheap "parlor trick" -- but is this always the case?

NOW YOU CAN LEARN THE ART OF LEVITATION

INVISIBILITY AND LEVITATION

Unknown to most people is the fact that just about anyone can levitate. You don't have to be a psychic. You don't have to have some kind of magical formula. All you have to know is the rules of levitation, and be willing to obey them.

Students of transcendental meditation are taught to levitate under the supervision of Maharishi Mahesh Yogi at his headquarters in Switzerland. On student described the experience this way: "People would rock gently, then more and more, then start lifting off into the air. You should really be in a lotus position to do it, you can hurt yourself landing if you've got a dangling undercarriage. To begin with it's like the Wright brothers' first flight, you come down with a bump. That's why we have to sit on foam rubber cushions. Then you learn to control it better, and it becomes totally exhilarating."

His Holiness Maharishi Mahesh offered his opinion on the human potential for levitation: "Yoga means union, the union of the individual awareness with the Unified Field of all the Laws of Nature in the state of Transcendental Consciousness. 'Yogic flying' demonstrates the ability of the individual to act from the Unified Field and enliven the total potential of Natural Law in all its expressions - mind, body, behavior, and environment. 'Yogic flying' presents in miniature the flight of galaxies in space, all unified in perfect order by natural law.

"The mind-body coordination displayed by 'Yogic Flying' shows that consciousness and its expression - the physiology- are in perfect balance. Scientific research has found maximum coherence in human brain functioning during 'Yogic Flying'. As the coherently functioning human brain is the unit of world peace, 'Yogic Flying' is the mechanics to make world peace a reality, and thereby bring world health, world happiness, world prosperity, a world free from suffering, heaven on earth in this generation."

INVISIBILITY AND LEVITATION

THE THREE STAGES OF YOGIC FLYING

According to the ancient Vedic texts, Yogic Flying develops in three stages, each representing a more refined style of physiological functioning. In the first stage, the body rises into the air in a series of short hops. This rising of the body involves no physical effort but merely a faint intention deep within the mind.

Even in its first state, the hopping stage, the practice of Yogic Flying creates waves of bubbling bliss in the consciousness and physiology of the practitioner. The mind-body coordination displayed by Yogic Flying shows that consciousness and its expression, the physiology, are in perfect balance. Scientific Research has found that there is maximum coherence in brain waves during Yogic Flying indicating highly orderly and holistic functioning of the brain.

In the second stage of Yogic Flying, the body rises into the air and remains there, floating. A number of Yogic Flyers have reported that they have risen into the air and remained there for a discernible moment before coming back down. In the third stage of Yogic Flying, the body flies through the air at will.

TM students insist that the only way to true weightlessness is through stringent mental training. Both physical and spiritual discipline is needed, they say. However, the feat is being accomplished countless times in homes, school yards, and in bars all over the world.

The phenomenon is simple to execute. The one to be levitated sits in a chair. Four people stand around him and place their index fingers in his armpits and in the crooks of his knees. Then they place their hands in a pile above his head, making sure that no one person's two hands are touching. The hands are interwoven. All four persons then concentrate deeply for about fifteen seconds. At a signal, the hands are then returned to the armpits and crooks of the knees of the subject, making sure that only the index fingers are used. At the count of three the subject can be easily lifted from the chair and into the air.

The person who is being levitated should not do anything to cooperate or resist. He should not become active in any way. The four standing persons should work in rhythm. Each participant should know what he has to do, and when he has to do it.

For instance, person Number One, standing at the seated person's right, should place his right hand on top of the seated person's head. Person Number Two, at right rear, places his right hand on top of Person Number One's right hand. Person Number Three, left rear, places his right hand on top of Person Number Two's right hand. Person Number Four places his right hand on top of the others. There are no four hands on top of one another. The process is now repeated, starting with Person Number One placing his left hand on top and continuing until all eight hands are in place. The movements should be practiced until everyone is in rhythm and there is an easy flow.

After the fifteen seconds of concentration, and when the person timing the event calls out, "Lift!" All four participants must place their forefingers as follows: Person one places his forefingers under the right knee of the seated subject. Person two places his forefingers under the right armpit. Person three places his fingers under the left armpit, and person four under the left knee. These movements should also be practiced until they are smooth and effortless.

Usually, there is a lot of giggling and laughing because the idea seems so absurd. However, it has been shown that after three or four attempts, when the chuckling has died down, there will usually be a measure of success.

INVISIBILITY AND LEVITATION

If done properly, it is actually possible to "lift" an individual by the use of just several fingers placed at specific pressure points on the body of the person to be levitated.

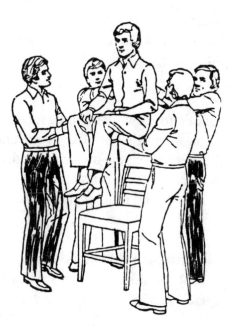

INVISIBILITY AND LEVITATION

Rhythm is important. So is practice. One Parapsychologist told me that he conducts the experiment in class quite frequently and has met with failure only once. In most cases the person who is levitated is raised about two to four feet in the air and experiences a feeling of lightness and exhilaration.

My friend also told me that after a lot of practice, it is no longer necessary to place four pairs of hands on top of the seated person's head. It seems that all that is necessary is for the four people to chant a phrase in unison five or six times. Any phrase will do. He said that "apple pie" is a good one. So is "vanilla sundae." Almost any innocuous phrase will do. The parapsychologist did emphasize that rhythm is extremely important. Levitation without it is impossible. If you do it with rhythm, there is little sensation of energy being expended.

CASES ARE RARE

According to the parapsychologist I spoke to, documentation on actual cases of levitation are rare, and that is because most of the claims are anecdotal and therefore not acceptable in scientific circles.

What that means is that there are a lot of stories, but no real proof. We mentioned earlier that Christ walked on water, that St. Joseph of Cupertino levitated, once as high as the topmost spires of St. Peter's Cathedral with hundreds watching. St. Teresa and St. John of the Cross levitated together right up to the ceiling. The scientists say that these are merely stories, and that all religions have them.

Some scientists are likely to make light of the subject by relating a Zen tale in which a disciple left his teacher to spend many years in solitary meditation. On his return, his guru asked him what he had learned. The disciple said proudly that he had learned to walk across the river on top of the water, to which the guru replied, "A pity. For one rupee the ferry will carry you across."

AN INDIAN YOGI LEVITATES WITH 150 WITNESSES

The date was June 6, 1936. The story and photos appeared in the *Illustrated London News*. The Indian yogi was Subbayah Pullavar. A witness, P.Y. Plunkett, stated: "The time was about 12:30PM and the sun directly above us so that shadows played no part in the performance. Standing quietly by was Subbayah Pullavar, the performer, with long hair, a drooping mustache and a wild look in his eye. He salaamed to us and stood chatting for awhile. He had been practicing this particular branch of yoga for nearly twenty years."

About 150 witnesses gathered about the performer. He began his ritual. Water was poured around the tent in which he was to levitate. Shoes with leather soles were banned inside the circle of water. The yogi entered the tent alone. Moments later aids removed the tent and there was the fakir suspended in the air about 36 inches from the ground. He held on to a cloth covered stick, but lightly and apparently only for balance and not for support. The manner in which he held the stick indicated that no exertion at all was being used. The space around and under the yogi was examined thoroughly, but the investigators could find no strings or any kind of invisible apparatus. The yogi was in a trance state. Photographs were taken from various angles during the four minutes the Indian was levitated.

Plunkett said that the tent was erected again so that the yogi could descend in private. However, Plunkett said he managed to witness it. "After about a minute," the witness said, "he appeared to away and then very slowly began to descend, still in a horizontal position. He took about five minutes to move from the top of the stick to the ground, a distance of about three feet. When Subbayah was back on the ground his assistants carried him over to where we were sitting and asked if we would try to bend his limbs. Even with assistance we were unable to do so." The Indian had to be splashed with water and rubbed for five minutes before he came around and was able to use his limbs.

THE BATCHELDOR REPORT

I've found that most parapsychologists believe that levitation is possible under controlled conditions. One experiment, apparently has truly achieved levitation. Written up in the September 1966 issue of the *Journal of the Society for Psychical Research*, the article was entitled: *Report on a Case of Table Levitation and Associated Phenomena.*

The author, British psychologist K. J. Batcheldor, says that he does not expect scientists to accept what he says at face value, but that he would be content if he succeeds in "inducing some few of my readers to suspend disbelief long enough to attempt sustained experimentations for themselves."

He means you and me. I've tried it, and it works exactly as Batheldor dictates. It can be done. Here's your chance to see how good you are.

LEVITATING A TABLE

Batcheldor learned that Tomas Faraday, the electrical wizard, had already known in 1853, that if a group of people sit at a table with their hands resting on its surface, the combined unconscious muscular action of the sitters can make the table tilt and dance. However, Batcheldor and his assistants were in for a surprise when they sat at a table in the spirit of amusement. He said the attitude "changed sharply in the eleventh meeting, when the table, instead of merely tilting or rocking on two legs, as it had done so far, rose clear from the floor. The explanation of unconscious muscle action was suddenly no longer applicable, since one cannot push a table up into the air, either consciously or unconsciously, when the hands are on top of it."

Batcheldor conducted 200 sittings in more than 18 months. He noted that in 80 of these sittings he was successful, and that in each case one of the sitters was a man named W. G. Chick. The phenomenon occurred only when Chick was at the table.

In my discussions with parapsychologists on this subject, I learned that they found the same truth in their experiments. One person, a medium or a sensitive, has the power to raise the table. If he or she is at the table, it will likely rise.

Batcheldor had another problem. The Early sittings were done in darkness, a fact which would have been pounded upon by skeptics. After the first levitation the table was equipped as follows:

"Four switches, one on each foot, were joined in a series to a battery lamp. . .The red lamp would light if, and only if, all four legs came off the floor. The apparatus stood up extremely well to the rough treatment it received during the more violent motions of the table, and a most vigorous deliberate rocking and tilting would not give a false signal."

The apparatus was used on tables ranging from two pounds to forty pounds. Batcheldor writes of the twelfth sitting when the apparatus was attached to a fifteen-pound table: "This twelfth meeting proved to be extremely colorful, containing the largest number of total levitations ever witnessed in one sitting. At first the table seemed to 'try out' the device 'tentatively' (it is difficult to resist such anthropomorphism). Gradually the movements became bolder and the lamp was lit for longer periods. By its red glow we could clearly see our hands on top of the table. The table then seemed to act as an excited person would, and proceeded to execute all manner of very lively movements - - - rocking, swaying, jumping, dancing, tilting, oscillating bodily both slowly and rapidly; it shook like a live thing even when totally levitated, almost shaking our hands off."

At this point in the amazing experiment, Batcheldor wanted to find out what the response would be if he issued vocal commands. He says: "Because the levitations were not very high, I said: 'Come on - - - higher!' At which the table rose up chest high and remained there for eight seconds. . .At one point the table levitated and floated right across the room. We had to leave our seats to follow it; it appeared to be about five inches off the floor, and the signal lamp remained alight until we crashed into some other furniture near the wall and the table dropped to the floor. When we reseated ourselves in the center of the room, the table soon came to life again, and took to rising up and then banging itself down with tremendous force, so that we feared it would break."

You might want to try this experiment with a group of friends. It's suggested that you use a light-weight table, like a bridge table, and insist that the group concentrate on levitating the table. The group should sit around the table and place their fingertips lightly on the surface of the table. Much like you would the pointer on a Ouija board.

It usually takes about ten to fifteen minutes of concentration before the table will start to respond. Sometimes it takes several sessions before any effect is noticed. It must be pointed out, however, that a dancing table, or tilting table, is not true levitation. It must rise off the floor with all four legs suspended in the air. A table that simply dances can be the result of unconscious muscular action in the hands.

EXPOSED: LEVITATION AND THE ANCIENT MASTERS OF WISDOM

INVISIBILITY AND LEVITATION

IS LEVITATION USEFUL?

Some experts feel that true levitation is associated only with those who are deeply religious. Nearly all sects can describe certain members who enjoyed the phenomenon. Aleister Crowley met a friend named Alan Bennett in 1902. Bennett had become a Buddhist monk and had become so weightless that he was blown about like leaf.

The French explorer, Alexandra David-Neel, tells of seeing a long-distance running by a Tibetan lama during the early part of the 20th Century. The explorer said that the Lama seemed to lift himself off the ground proceeding by leaps. It was as though he had been endowed with the elasticity of a ball and rebounded each time his feet touched the ground. He ran with the regularity of a pendulum. He is said to have run hundreds of miles using this strange form of locomotion, keeping his eyes fixed on some far-distant goal.

Nijinsky, the famed Russian ballet dancer, also had the unique ability of appearing to be almost weightless. He would leap high and fall slowly, like a feather, in what was known as the slow vault.

The noted fortean writer John Keel in his book, *Jadoo* (Gilbert Press), told about his strange meeting in Tibet with a timid little lama named Nyang-Pas. Keel had heard that Nyang-Pas was a great Siddha, someone who can perform miracles. The lama however, denied it. "I am just a simple lama, I only practice the teachings of my religion."

When Keel asked Nyang-Pas if he could be taught something, the lama said: "It would take you a lifetime of solitude. . .but perhaps I can introduce you to the principle." John Keel takes up the story: "He struggled to his feet, pressed one hand on the top of his walking stick, a heavy branch about four feet long, frowned a little with effort, and then slowly lifted his legs up off the floor until he was sitting cross-legged in the air. There was nothing behind him or under him. His sole support was his stick, which he seemed to use to keep his balance."

"Can you teach me this?" Keel asked.

"No," came the reply, "it is not something you can learn overnight, it is a matter of will. But there are other things, basic things, for example, think of an object, some common thing."

Keel thought of a tree, the lama gazed deep into his eyes and smiled.

"That is too easy. You are thinking of a tree, try something else."

Next Keel thought of an old pair of boots. Again, the lama guessed correctly.

Again Keel asked to be taught the secrets, but the lama told him he would have to learn for himself with practice. His instructions were simple, first Keel had to cleanse his mind of all thoughts and concentrate entirely on his subject. If the subject is a reasonably intelligent person, able to visualize strongly the object he is thinking of, an image of that object would pop into Keels mind.

The object must be visualized. Words can't be intercepted by a novice telepath. And disciplined people tend to think in words rather than in images. As for levitation, Nyang-Pas explained that it takes a very high form of concentration, separating mental vision from the body, till the body becomes lighter then air.

INVISIBILITY AND LEVITATION

AN ANCIENT ART

Research into this fascinating subject has brought us into contact with literature on the ancients, who apparently had mastered levitation to a far greater degree than we moderns. Enormous earthworks, for instance, in England and the desert patterns in Peru, had to have been accomplished by people who could levitate easily. The white horse at Uffington in Oxfordshire is carved on terrain so hilly that it can be appreciated only from the air, indicating that only levitators could have designed it.

The ancient Druids allegedly could fly at will, yet there is some feeling among the experts that they may have flown in out-of-body experiments rather than actual physical flight.

Those who have truly accomplished the art of levitation say that with few exceptions the phenomenon requires training and discipline for a long period of time. There is a mysterious law at work, a law that says the body will be given permission to defy the law of gravity.

Spontaneous or random levitations may also work on this principle. The levitator may accidentally stumble upon the natural ability that permits them to rise into the air. Investigator Charles Fort, who wrote huge volumes of strange events during the early part of this century came across a case of a 12-year old boy named Henry Jones from Shepton Mallet in England who rose to the ceiling on several occasions. The year was 1657. At one time the boy was observed sailing over a garden wall. The distance was 30 yards. If he knew the secret formula, it didn't last long for him. After one year he lost his ability to levitate. Afterwards he was shunned by the townspeople who believed him bewitched.

INVISIBILITY AND LEVITATION

A FIRST HAND EXPERIENCE

"My sensation was that of being lighter than the air. No pressure on any part of the body, no unconsciousness or entrancement. From the position of the mark on the wall, it is clear that my head must have been close to the ceiling. The ascent, of which I was perfectly conscious, was very gradual and steady, not unlike that of being in a elevator, but without any perceptible sensation of motion other than that of feeling lighter than the atmosphere, of being completely free."

That is a description of how it feels to experience the phenomenon of levitation, the rising of ones physical body against the natural force of gravitation. It is particularly noteworthy because the narrator was William Stainton Moses, a most remarkable English religious figure, medium, and psychical researcher. He was one of the founding members of the British Society for Psychical Research, and a man of such unquestionable integrity that Andrew Lang, in discussing the possibility of fraud in some of Moses's phenomena, said that "the choice was between a moral and a physical miracle."

W. Stainton Moses was levitated a number of times in front of respectable witnesses. On one occasion he was swept up from his feet, thrown onto a large table and then onto an adjacent sofa. Though it seemed to the others present that a tremendous amount of force was involved, Moses suffered no injury whatsoever.

The nature of levitation suggests that the ability may draw upon the same source of energy as does poltergeist activity. We understand now that the poltergeist is a purely natural phenomenon centering around a target subject who is often a juvenile at the age of puberty, or someone experiencing great stress and mental anguish.

It seems reasonable to suppose that the force emanating from the target subject, in a manner science does not fully understand, and capable of moving relatively heavy objects such as furniture could, if directed toward the ground, effectively lift that subject's body into the air.

We find levitation associated with a few poltergeist cases, though sometimes it is not the target subject who is lifted up. The classic case of the Epworth Vicarage Poltergeist is an example. Nancy Wesley, daughter of the Vicar, was often elevated in the presence of her four sisters. However, the available evidence in this case is that the target subject was sister Hetty.

HOLDING ON

It has been said that some who levitate are able to extend their power to others who hold them by the hand. This is questionable. It seems more likely that it is just impossible to overcome the levitating force. Harry Keller, the stage magician who, before Houdini's time, investigated the claims of many mediums, witnessed and inadvertently participated in a levitation of the medium William Eglinton.

Keller wrote for the **Proceedings** of the **SPR**, "I was placed on Mr. Eglinton's left and seized his left hand firmly in mine . . . I felt him rise slowly in the air and as I retained firm hold of his hand, I was pulled to my feet, and subsequently compelled to jump on a chair and then on the table in order to retain my hold on him. That his body did ascend in the air on that occasion with an apparent disregard for the law of gravity, there can be no doubt." Keller added that his own body appeared to have been rendered non-susceptible to gravity as he felt the levitating effects of the medium.

There are some recorded instances when a weight loss of a levitator is immediately evident to witnesses. In Grenoble, France, a girl given to ecstatic trances became so stiff and light at times that it was possible to lift her from the ground by merely holding her elbow. A very unusual case was that of Frau Frederica Hauffe, the famous Seeress of Prevorst. According to Dr. Justinus Kerner, the man who investigated the remarkable powers that centered around her, while she was in a trance she was put into a bath where she floated like a cork to the top of the water. Dr. Kerner reported that if he placed his hand against hers, he could draw her up from the ground as if he were a magnet.

GRAVITY WAVE

At first glance, cases such as these seem to suggest that weight, as if it were a substantial, corporeal entity, had been withdrawn from the body. However, this is not the proper way to look at the situation. Weight is not such an energy, weight is the quality of a reaction. That is, weight is the reaction of a mass to the gravitational attraction of another mass. When we weigh something, we are not weighing something tangible, but rather the reaction of that thing to the gravitational pull of the Earth.

It would seem, then, that somewhere between the center of gravity of a levitator and the center of gravity of the Earth, a line of force is set up that has the effect of neutralizing the pull of gravity on all other points in the elevated body. For some years now, Dr. Joseph Weber of the University of Maryland has been experimenting with something called a gravity wave. Scientists have observed that the laws that govern electrostatic attraction, electromagnetic waves, and gravity, seem to act as if they were manifestations of some greater general law. This is the Unified Field Theory that Albert Einstein was working on at the time of his death. He sought one law that would apply to all of those similar phenomenon so that interaction between them could be studied.

It is entirely within the realm of possibility that a link may exist between the gravity wave and certain waves generated in the nervous system of the human body. Dr. Weber's work indicates the gravitational wave has a frequency of 1600 cycles per second. A wave generated at the same rate, but out of phase with the gravity wave, would neutralize it. This could produce buoyancy, but not levitation.

However, if a brain wave or a nervous system wave, out of phase with the gravity wave to the proper degree were generated, then the force of gravity would theoretically be overcome. According to this idea, electric waves generated within the levitator would oppose the force of gravity along a thin line extending between their center of gravity and that of the Earth.

The one thing that stands out in all levitation cases is that the levitator was in an altered state of consciousness. It seems clear that the ecstatic reaches levitation through meditation of an intense sort. The medium achieves something similar by deliberately going into trance. The medium Willi Schneider used to increase his breath rate to about 75 per minute to achieve trance. It is interesting that at that rate, both heartbeat and breath would probably be synchronized. Levitation then, seems to depend upon a trance or altered mental state of consciousness. Breathing exercises are apparently one means of approaching this phenomenon.

COULD SOUND BE A KEY TO LEVITATION?

Richard Clark, PhD gives the following explanation in a chapter he wrote for the book *Anti-Gravity and The World Grid* (Adventures Unlimited Press): "We know from the priests of the Far East that they were able to lift heavy boulders up high mountains with the help of groups of various sounds . . . the knowledge of the various vibrations in the audio range demonstrates to a scientist of physics that a vibrating and condensed sound field can nullify the power of gravity.

INVISIBILITY AND LEVITATION

"The following is based on observations which were made in Tibet. I have this report from civil engineer and flight manager, Henry Kjelson, a friend of mine. He later on included this in his book, *The Lost Techniques*. A Swedish doctor, Dr. Jarl, a friend of Kjelsons, studied at oxford. During those times he became friends with a young Tibetan student. In 1939, Dr. Jarl made a journey to Egypt for the English Scientific Society. There he was seen by a messenger of his Tibetan friend, and urgently requested to come to Tibet to meet a high Lama.

"Dr. Jarl followed the messenger and arrived after a long journey by plane and yak caravans through the mountains, at the monastery, where the old Lama and his friend who was now holding a high position were living. Dr. Jarl stayed in Tibet for some time, and because of his friendship with the Tibetans he learned a lot of things that other foreigners had no chance to hear about, or observe.

"One day his friend took him to a place in the neighborhood of the monastery and showed him a sloping meadow which was surrounded in the north west by high cliffs. In one of the rock walls, at a height of about 250 meters, was a huge hole which looked like the entrance to a cave. In front of this hole there was a platform on which the monks were building a rock wall. The only access to this platform was from the top of the cliff and the monks lowered themselves down with the help of ropes.

"In the middle of the meadow, about 250 meters from the cliff, was a polished slab of rock with a bowl-like cavity in the center. The bowl had a diameter of one meter and a depth of 15 centimeters. A block of stone was maneuvered into the cavity by yak oxen. The block was one meter wide and one and one-half meters long. Then nineteen musical instruments were set in an arc of ninety degrees at a distance of sixty three meters from the stone slab. The radius of 63 meters was measured out accurately. The musical instruments consisted of thirteen drums and six trumpets.

"The drums were made up of eight large drums, four medium sized drums, and one small drum. The big drums and all the trumpets were fixed on mounts which would be adjusted with staffs in the direction of the slab of stone. The drums were made of 3mm thick sheet iron, and had a weight of 150 kg. They were built in five sections. All the drums were open at one end, while the other end had a bottom of metal, on which the monks beat with big leather clubs. Behind each instrument was a row of monks.

"When the stone was in position, the monk behind the small drum gave a signal to start. The small drum had a very sharp sound, and could be heard even with the other instruments making a terrible din. All the monks were singing and chanting a prayer, slowly increasing the tempo of this unbelievable noise. During the first four minutes nothing happened, then as the speed of the drumming, and the noise, increased, the big stone block started to rock and sway, and suddenly it took off into the air with an increasing speed in the direction of the platform in front of the cave hole 250 meters high. After three minutes of ascent it landed on the platform.

"Continuously, they brought new blocks to the meadow, and the monks using this method, transported five to six blocks per hour on a parabolic flight track approximately 500 meters long and 250 meters high. From time to time, a stone split, and the monks moved the split stones away."

The report concludes by noting that to prove he was not going mad, the doctor made two different films of the levitation. The society for which Dr. Jarl was working for, confiscated the movies and declared them classified. To this day, the films have not been released for public viewing.

Bruce Cathie has spent a good part of his life working with mathematics and mapping the Earth's energy grid systems. He offers a good explanation for levitation based upon his research as well as the investigations of others:

INVISIBILITY AND LEVITATION

"The sound waves being generated by the combination of instruments were directed in such a way that an anti-gravitational effect was created at the center of focus (position of the stones) and around the periphery, or the arc, of a third of a circle through which the stones moved."

Cathie concludes that the Tibetans as well as the Egyptians, and possibly the original inhabitants of Atlantis "had possession of the secrets relating to the geometric structure of matter, and the methods of manipulating the harmonic values." Cathie believes that the Tibetans were able to defy the laws of gravity and actually possessed devices which could travel through the air as if they were weightless. He believes that by studying ancient records, we may soon be able to construct a type of "flying saucer" or floating disc of our own that will be the forerunner of humankind actually learning to levitate objects, as well as ourselves, on a permanent basis.

THE INCREDIBLE POWERS OF BORIS ERMOLAEV

The iron curtain has been down for a number of years. The Soviet Union no longer exists. Information that had once been forbidden has now become available to those seeking the truth. However, despite the new freedoms enjoyed by the people of Russia, some things still remain a mystery.

Take for instance the strange powers of Boris Ermolaev. At one time the Russian film director's exploits filled Soviet scientific journals. Now however, Ermolaev has faded back into obscurity, with no easy answers to his unusual powers. Soviet scientists were convinced that Ermolaev had genuine paranormal abilities. Genady Sergeyev, a doctor of engineering and a consultant mathematician was certain of Ermolaev's powers: "Ermolaev has the unusual ability of concentrating his energy into a focal point in mid-air and causing objects to be suspended in the air for many seconds."

131

INVISIBILITY AND LEVITATION

Professor Venyamin Pushkin has worked several times with Ermolaev in carefully controlled government authorized experiments. Pushkin wrote in a scientific journal, "There are actually people who possess the capacity of influencing objects so that they remain suspended in mid-air. I have witnessed Ermolaev suspend objects in mid-air. I believe this man is capable of creating a magnetic field that defies gravity."

The experiments took place in 1973 and 1974 in laboratories at Moscow University. Pushkin published an official report in which he said that each experiment was preceded by warm-up exercises so that Ermolaev could reach a state of high tension.

When this was done, Ermolaev started with simple demonstrations. He placed his hands over a spread-out deck of cards, face down, and correctly named each card's suit and value. Ermolaev then moved objects on a table without touching them. After that he attacked the major part of his experiment. Pushkin wrote: "Ermolaev took an object in his hands, pressed it between his outstretched hands, then slowly moved his hands apart. The object remained hanging in mid-air. He continued to move his hands till each palm was about eight inches clear of the object. It remained in mid-air for a number of seconds."

Another authority who witnessed Ermolaev at work was Ivan Guderman, science editor of the newspaper *Evening Sverdlosk*. Guderman has made numerous important contributions to psychic research. He was permitted to view some of the experiments that took place.

"The room is empty except for a table in the middle. On it, a ping-pong ball, a box of matches, and several pencils. A man walks into the room, stops in front of the table, stretches out his hand, freezes, but by the expression on his face, by the tension of his body, one knows that he just doesn't stand there, he is working.

INVISIBILITY AND LEVITATION

"A minute goes by, another. Suddenly the ball is jerked from its position and is rolling off the table. The box is also moving, as though sliding across the surface of the table. The pencils seem to have lost their gravity and have risen into the air."

What is Ermolaev's magic? Pushkin's original thought was that static electricity played a part. The electrical charges made the objects move. Further experiments, however, proved that such was not the case. There was no way that static electricity could make pencils levitate. Pushkin then wrote in his report:

"I then considered the theory of one of our scientists, A.P. Dubrov. Its essence is that living systems are capable of originating and receiving gravitational waves. To accept this, one must accept the most unusual assumption that man is able to give birth to a gravitational field and then, with its help, affect surrounding objects. I was able to cross-check this theory with the strong evidence offered in the experiments with Ermolaev."

Pushkin stressed the point that it was merely theoretical that Ermolaev was able to create gravitational fields. He wrote: "The tradition of science invokes certain taboos in areas that deal with a violation of fundamental laws of nature. The ability of man to affect objects near him is still considered by numbers of scientists as something pertaining to violation of the basic laws of nature. However, what is essential and should be stressed time and time again is that feats of moving and suspending objects in the air, with all their unusual and mind-boggling aspects, do not contradict the existing framework of physics.

Ermolaev has also levitated people. One was a famous Russian actress who preferred not to have her name mentioned. With a small audience watching, Ermolaev lifted her about four feet into the air while she was in a prone position. He managed to keep her suspended for about 20 seconds.

INVISIBILITY AND LEVITATION

No one to date has quite explained to any satisfaction how Boris Ermolaev was able to create levitation. What is known is that when he levitated anything, either an object or a person, he suffered extreme trauma. His body would tremble, he would sweat, his heart rate would increase, his concentration reached a depth that most of us can never attain. He was totally immersed in what he was doing.

Those who have mastered the phenomenon, like Boris Ermolaev, say it is much easier to levitate objects that are light in weight. The suggestion is that you try it with pencils, paper clips and rubber bands. Move those objects before you try to levitate yourself.

Concentration is the key. Have absolutely no distractions. Do it alone so that you won't feel self-conscious. Once your thoughts start to wander, take a break. Concentrate in short periods of time until you can increase the span.

When you have mastered the light objects, try levitating a bridge table. Remember, table tipping is not levitation. The table must rise straight up, with all four legs off the floor. It helps if you are psychic. Most likely you know that you are, but are not sure to what extent. There are no measurements. Levitation may let you know just how psychic you really are.

Perhaps Ermolaev had discovered the secrets of the Siddha's. The ancient wisdom that only the dedicated could ever dream of mastering. To know such secrets would take years of spiritual quests and mental mastery. Or maybe Ermolaev was born with the natural ability of levitation already in place, ready to go at the slightest need. Maybe the Saints and other Holy men who levitated during religious ecstasy were also such "naturals." These natural powers could also act as a beacon to those who have the ability to "see" such energy in humans.

STRANGE MYSTERY OF PSYCHIC DIANE TESSMAN

INVISIBILITY AND LEVITATION

Diane Tessman has certainly led an interesting life. She spent 11 years of her life as a school teacher. She has lived in the Virgin Islands, Florida and now resides in St. Ansgar, Iowa where she devotes much of her time to New Age activities.

Diane has her own New Age Church and channels a future human known to her as Tibus. Diane is of the opinion that Tibus channels only through her, although she has channeled other beings including, extraterrestrials, devas, angels, and Goddesses.

According to Diane, 1980 was an active one for her psychically. There were all sorts of space contacts which made themselves known to her in creative ways. For instance, in the spring of that year - May 9th to be exact -her smoke alarm started to buzz off and on. The batteries were fresh and she was not cooking at the time. The off-and-on buzzing sounded much like Morse Code. Unfortunately, Diane did not know how to read the code. She did, however, take note of the time. It was 7:35 AM.

Later, when she turned on her radio, she learned that a large ship had rammed the Skyway Bridge, which stretches over Tampa Bay near St. Petersburg, Florida. Cars and buses plunged 100 feet down into the waters, killing 33 people. The time of the accident? 7:35 AM. Diane said that she feels that because she was living close to the disaster at the time, that the souls which had been torn so suddenly from their bodies had provided the energy that was manifested in the bussing of the smoke alarm.

Incidents like this one piled up during the spring and summer of 1980 and apparently prepared her for an experience she will never forget as long as she lives. Diane related her experience this way: "One night soon after I had gone to bed (I was not dreaming), I levitated through the wall: My mind was not on my space contacts and I was not meditating. I was casually churning over the worldly events of the day which had been very 'humdrum' and typical. I was lying on my stomach, as is my habit, when I abruptly felt my body rise up several feet above the bed! There was a choppy, rippling sensation much like one feels riding on an air mattress in slightly rough waters at the beach. Usually, I am not frightened when paranormal events occur or when I spot a UFO or receive a telepathic message; in fact, I long for these phenomena to occur."

Placed under hypnosis by Dr. Leo Sprinkle of the University of Wyoming, Diane Tessman recalled being abducted on board a craft from outer space at the age of six or seven. Later in life she was to experience an ongoing choir of unexplainable events including being levitated and partially pulled through a solid wall. Diane said that the sudden levitation did scare her and that she wasn't sure why until she realized that she was frightened because she was floating free through space. Now, something else had control. Upon reflection, Diane said: "Perhaps I needed a lesson in humility and trust."

Still, her experience was far from over. "I was just attempting to logically figure out my predicament without too much panic and terror, when my entire body made an abrupt right angle turn, feet first. With my last shred of calm rationale, I realized that my feet now had to be outside the wall! My single bed sat flush against an outside wall of the house. There was no room for my body to be turned sideways and still be totally within my house!"

Was it an astral journey? Diane thinks not. She has had many of them and they were never like this. She does believe that she was levitated and taken somewhere, but she has no memory of the trip. She remembers rising up from the bed and then being outside the wall and trying desperately to get back inside.

Says Diane: "I had great difficulty in getting my eyes open. It was a very strange feeling because it seemed that I had two sets of eyes; I could open one set with great effort but they would not function, could not see the reality I had come from but only a calm, black, other-dimensional place. Finally, after several minutes of attempting to fight panic and asserting my own will with all my strength, my 'other' set of eyes opened and I was back in bed."

INVISIBILITY AND LEVITATION

Again, Diane thinks the adventure may have been brought about to teach her humility, trust and faith. In any event, she had a similar experience several weeks later, and had the same terrified reaction. "This time," says Diane, "I was lying on my back, eyes open and totally awake. Just as before. Without warning my bed began to dump me out the wall! I remember realizing that I was totally outside the wall...and then I have no recollection of events until I desperately struggled to return to my bed."

There was a bizarre piece of physical evidence accompanying both weird abductions. The battery of her car parked outside the house was drained on both occasions. In many UFO encounters, car batteries and their casings are damaged or ruined because of the strong electromagnetic fields around UFOs. These fields usually destroy batteries and car ignition systems.

On the surface it appeared that Diane Tessman levitated and perhaps also became invisible. Slipping through the wall tells us that there must have been some sort of invisibility involved (either of her or the wall). Up till this point in her life, this remarkable woman had touched on all phases of the paranormal except levitation and invisibility. Could it be that her other-dimensional contacts now wanted her to become proficient in these arts as well?

What we do know about Diane Tessman is that the longer you are in her company the more certain you are that she is a woman who has touched the unkown. She has also come in physical contact with other-world aliens - - - and has the scar to prove it.

DIANE'S VISIBLE ENIGMA

Diane has a scar that runs between her nose and lip. It is extremely straight. The scar is so deep that the tissue goes all the way through to the inside of her mouth.

INVISIBILITY AND LEVITATION

Diane has had it nearly all of her life. She doesn't know how she got it. She has investigated every possibility. Her mother insists that Diane never cut herself there as a child and never has had even minor corrective surgery. Diane has checked with the hospital, but there is no record of any extra expense for facial surgery. The scar itself looks exactly like it was done by a surgeon's scalpel, yet no one in her family can remember such an operation.

Diane also noted that the scar is in the exact spot in which a surgeon would cut if he wanted to enter the brain with a scalpel or a laser beam. The procedure eliminates the barrier that the skull represents. Was her scar placed there by UFO beings during one of her abductions? Diane Tessman can't be sure, although she does feel that she has had psychic surgery of some kind, and with a purpose that is beyond her.

"While many of those in contact with Higher Realms do not have unknown scars, others of us do," Diane points out. "The Star Children are the ones who have the majority of scars, due to surgery in early childhood or blood or tissue samples taken in early childhood abductions. It is not an honor nor a disgrace to have a scar due to your contact with UFO beings or with Higher Realms. We all have diverse and unique purposes on our survival path through the turmoil of the End Days. All of us are equal and all of us are One."

Are there any good explanations to account for the strange powers of invisibility and levitation? It is conceivable that there isn't any one process by which these abilities take place. Any breakthrough in our understanding of these powers will come only when the scientific community can observe and study human invisibility and levitation in controlled conditions.

Unfortunately, there are few contemporary psychics who seem capable of reproducing these feats in the laboratory. Perhaps our only alternative lies in the mystic East, with some yogic master who would be willing to demonstrate his abilities under careful scientific scrutiny. If it is pursued, it may only be a short time before mankind is able to learn levitation as easily as you could learn the technique of hypnotism. Then, and only then will these amazing powers be understood and developed, hopefully for the betterment of all mankind.

ADDITIONAL BEST SELLERS BY "COMMANDER X"
A FORMER MILITARY INTELLIGENCE OPERATIVE SPEAKS OUT!

COSMIC PATRIOT FILES
From the "Committee of 12 to Save the Earth"

2 VOLUME SET

THE ULTIMATE DECEPTION

UNDERGROUND ALIEN BASES

NIKOLA TESLA—FREE ENERGY AND THE WHITE DOVE

THE CONTROLLERS

THE PHILADELPHIA EXPERIMENT CHRONICLES—EXPLORING THE STRANGE CASE OF ALFRED BIELEK & DR. M.K. JESSUP

b